Teaching Social Justice

Teaching Social Justice

Critical Tools for the Intercultural Communication Classroom

Brandi Lawless and Yea-Wen Chen

ROWMAN & LITTLEFIELD
Lanham • Boulder • New York • London

Published by Rowman & Littlefield
An imprint of The Rowman & Littlefield Publishing Group, Inc.
4501 Forbes Boulevard, Suite 200, Lanham, Maryland 20706
www.rowman.com

6 Tinworth Street, London SE11 5AL, United Kingdom

Copyright © 2021 by The Rowman & Littlefield Publishing Group, Inc.

All rights reserved. No part of this book may be reproduced in any form or by any electronic or mechanical means, including information storage and retrieval systems, without written permission from the publisher, except by a reviewer who may quote passages in a review.

British Library Cataloguing in Publication Information Available

Library of Congress Cataloging-in-Publication Data

Names: Lawless, Brandi, author. | Chen, Yea-Wen, author.
Title: Teaching social justice : critical tools for the intercultural communication classroom / Brandi Lawless and Yea-Wen Chen.
Description: Lanham, Maryland : Rowman & Littlefield, 2021. | Includes bibliographical references and index. | Summary: "This pedagogical guide presents conceptual overviews, student activities, and problem-solving strategies for teaching intercultural communication. The authors navigate eight categories of potential conflict, including: communicating power and privilege, engagement in social justice, and assessing intercultural pedagogies for social justice" — Provided by publisher.
Identifiers: LCCN 2021014635 (print) | LCCN 2021014636 (ebook) |
  ISBN 9781538121344 (cloth) | ISBN 9781538121351 (paperback) |
  ISBN 9781538121368 (ebook)
Subjects: LCSH: Social justice and education. | Intercultural Communication—Study and teaching. | Classroom environment—Social aspects.
Classification: LCC LC192.2 .L38 2021 (print) | LCC LC192.2 (ebook) |
  DDC 370.11/5—dc23
LC record available at https://lccn.loc.gov/2021014635
LC ebook record available at https://lccn.loc.gov/2021014636

This book is dedicated to the teachers who have transformed our lives—especially Professor Mary Jane Collier for her endless support, critical love, and modeling of what it means to be an intercultural communication teacher and scholar with a heart for social justice.

Contents

Acknowledgments	ix
Introduction	1
1 Articulating Philosophies and Assumptions	17
2 Communicating Power and Privilege	27
3 Negotiating Avowed and Ascribed Identities for Social Justice	41
4 Building Alliances	55
5 Community Engagement for Social Justice	65
6 Deconstructing Ideologies	75
7 Thinking and Acting Globally	89
8 "Assessing" Intercultural Pedagogies for Social Justice	101
Conclusions and Reflections: Teaching Social Justice in a Changing and Challenging Moment	111
Appendices A–N: Critical Intercultural Communication Activities	119
Glossary	159
Notes	161
References	163
Index	177
About the Authors	187

Acknowledgments

We would like to thank everyone who made this book possible. First, thank you to all intercultural communication teacher-scholars who trusted us to participate in our research and share their experiences, which laid the foundation for this book. Additionally, we have a deep appreciation for the work of the scholars who contributed to the *Stories from the Field* sections of this book: Drs. Lindsay Scott, Anjana Mudambi, Gust Yep, Alberto González, Mary Jane Collier, Sara DeTurk, Godfried Asante, Kathryn Sorrells, and John Oetzel. Thank you! We could not have finished this project without the help of our research assistant, Ariel Wei. Ariel, thank you for your feedback and attention to detail. Thank you to Grace Wakefield for early editing and feedback. We have immense gratitude for the reviewers who gave initial feedback on our book proposal. Moreover, thanks to our students and colleagues who inspire/d us to do this work. Every conversation we have had about teaching and learning this subject, at conferences and in the classroom, informed the scope of this project.

Finally, our deepest thanks go to our families for their unwavering support. Thanks to our partners (Nathan and Masato) and to our sons (Griffin and Leo), who allowed us to make this commitment in time and effort during a difficult time in our global society. Yea-Wen would like to extend her gratitude and appreciation toward her Agōng (陳乾), Amà (陳儉), and parents (陳承財 and 吳秀況) in Taiwan for supporting her decision to stay and work in U.S. academia. We love you!

Introduction

I was raised by a single mother in rural Pennsylvania. At a young age, I was interpellated into discourses that defined me as less than, poor, ugly, and dirty. I developed tactics for nonverbally communicating that I was on "the list" for free lunches to the cafeteria cashier, and seamlessly buying groceries with my mother's EBT card. Discussions about class were off-limits, "family business," but that rule didn't stop me from seeing and hiding from a set of discourses that would, for some, define who I was and what I was capable of doing. Though not a first-generation college student (because my mom went back to school in her thirties), I was only the second person in my family to choose to further my education. I struggled as I was told that I lack the knowledge and capability necessary to succeed. I persisted. I was the first in my family to pursue graduate school. It was then that I discovered intercultural communication, a way of understanding myself, a means of hope, and a professional future. Likewise, my introduction to critical communication pedagogy changed my perspective on education. I started to reflect inward and relate outward. In utilizing critical pedagogies in the Intercultural Communication classroom, I have heard many stories that articulate the challenges of living at the intersections and on the margins and have worked with students to push back against the systems that perpetuate these obstacles. After being the target of a right-wing media attack for publishing work about emotional labor for women (especially women of color), the personal became even more political. The exigence for articulating critical intercultural communication pedagogies became apparent. Instructors who teach at these intersections need support as they wade through turbulent tides of speaking truth to power and teaching critically. I am writing this book with Yea-Wen because I believe we have much to learn from each other and much to offer together.

As we deeply reflect on our teaching, politics, and theoretical foundations, we can further work toward education as a practice of freedom.

As an immigrant woman faculty of color growing up in Taiwan and living in San Diego, my journey of learning and teaching in U.S. academia has been both empowering and disempowering. When I entered U.S. academia in the fall of 2004, I was a racially aware but unconscious international graduate student of color who called herself "Rita" and was dating, and supported by, an older white U.S. American man I met in Taipei, Taiwan. Today, I identify myself as a politically Taiwanese and culturally Chinese immigrant woman working to reclaim and embrace much of my cultural wealth that has been undervalued, ridiculed, marginalized, and Othered throughout my learning and teaching experiences in both Taiwan and the United States (e.g., my heritage as a granddaughter of a Taoist oracle). As a first-generation college student and faculty, I would not be where I am today without all the mentors, allies, and friends who saw and see the potential in me when I struggle(d) with feeling like an "imposter." I was first introduced to critical pedagogy when I took a critical race theory seminar with Dr. Ricky Lee Allen at the University of New Mexico. Increasingly, I see the work that I do with students inside and outside the classroom as a central site in which I do the work of a (critical) intercultural communication teacher-scholar. I am writing this book with Brandi because this work is deeply personal and political to me as a human being, as an educator, as a mother-scholar, and more. Fundamentally, I believe in education as a tool of liberation when it is done with an equity mindset, a cultural asset view of difference, and a deep commitment to social justice.

Rooted in intercultural communication, this book sits and situates itself at an interdisciplinary intersection of communication, critical communication pedagogy, and social justice education. At its core, we develop in this book that teaching intercultural communication for social justice is to embrace and put into practice the commitments of critical intercultural communication pedagogy. Furthermore, practicing social justice in the Intercultural Communication classroom is defined by and constituted in the moments of how instructors and students have the important yet challenging conversations. Intercultural Communication, one of the most frequently offered courses in communication studies (Bertelsen & Goodboy, 2009), is positioned within a broader discourse about how students and wider college communities approach and understand "diversity" on campus. As a signifier, the word "diversity" connotes, conjures up, and signals a wide range of related issues such as cultural sensitivity, difference, inclusion, equity, and social justice. Its relatively fluid, unstable, and slippery nature is probably why "diversity" is preferred over terms such as social justice by many colleges and universities.

For example, at the University of San Francisco (where Brandi teaches) Intercultural Communication fulfills the Core E: Social Sciences requirement and the CD: Cultural Diversity requirement for all undergraduate students. At San Diego State University (where Yea-Wen teaches), Intercultural Communication, designated as a "cultural diversity course," fulfills the Social and Behavioral component (area B) of the Explorations of Human Experience requirement in general education for all undergraduate students. At the University of New Mexico, where we both taught the course during graduate school, Intercultural Communication was a diversity requirement for all students entering health professions (e.g., pre-med, dental, nursing) and was a requirement for undergraduate majors. These are only a few examples, but the positioning of Intercultural Communication as a required or recommended course is widespread. The utility of the course seems to be acknowledged outside of the communication discipline in that all students should be expected to learn how to communicate with individuals from diverse backgrounds and about diverse groups of people.

Our approach to teaching intercultural communication is guided by principles of critical communication pedagogy (Fassett & Warren, 2007). Through this lens, we take a praxical approach to the classroom in which theories of identity, power, institutional influence, and hegemony should not only be taught and deconstructed but also inform the curriculum development, student-instructor communication, and educational philosophies. We see communication in education not as a transactional process, but rather a co-created process with the potential for fundamental transformation (Freire, 1970).

Of all the interwoven contexts in which teaching and learning intercultural communication occurs, we must acknowledge and highlight the particular context of neoliberalism in higher education. The university has become a marketplace of ideas, meaning that any student should be able to find their idea on a shelf and see it as equal to other ideas or opinions. This becomes a challenge in the Intercultural Communication classroom, where we encourage students to speak from experiences with regard to their multiple, intersectional identities or from places of vulnerability. Moreover, the drive to make instructors teach more students with the same or less amount of resources constricts instructors' ability to build relationships and attend to the sensitive and personal issues that arise in a class focused on cultures. Contingent, non-tenure-track, and pre-tenure faculty often have to weigh their desire to push students to think critically and feel productive discomfort with the effect on their teaching evaluations and job security. For these reasons, understanding the ideological and political contexts in which we teach this course informs *how* we teach these challenging and important topics.

Our framework includes discussions of *social justice*, *equity*, and *intercultural communication*. In a recent forum on identifying key intercultural urgencies, issues, and challenges, Alexander, Arasaratnam, Durham et al. (2014) note, "While such buzzwords as social justice and social responsibility are frequently mentioned in the recent literature, intercultural communication scholarship has rarely explored the context-specific meanings and different behavioral manifestations of these supposedly sharable values" (p. 60). We agree that intercultural communication scholars need to work on specifying and concretizing our core and sharable values. In this work, we approach social justice as both the goal and process of co-creating spaces for individuals and groups to speak their truths on their own terms and be heard; relentlessly striving for equitable distribution of and access to resources; persisting to recognize and challenge power imbalances that organize everyday communication interactions; and practicing actions to bring about positive changes in society. Through a lens of social justice, we view communication "is/as activism" (Alexander, Arasaratnam, Durham et al., 2014). This definition of social justice is important in intercultural communication work because we need to better understand how transforming our communication with others has the potential to trigger, instigate, and create larger structural change.

We view diversity as the context that supports and sometimes mandates courses like Intercultural Communication. At the same time, we recognize that *diversity* is a neoliberal term that has been co-opted to reproduce group stereotypes (primarily racial as well as intersectional), and has contributed to Othering communities that are already under-resourced, underrepresented, and marginalized. The rhetoric of diversity has been used to create boxes and quotas that need to be filled with certain bodies (in the seats and in the front of the classroom), or "celebrate" culture while actually exoticizing cultural differences. This understanding of diversity can lead to neoliberal multiculturalism—the active recruitment of a diverse campus body without the resources needed to succeed (Lawless & Chen, 2017). This view of diversity is meritocratic in that it simultaneously touts individualism while ignoring individual differences (Darder, 2012).

Departing from institutional preference for the term "diversity," we choose social justice and equity intentionally. Ahmed (2007) argues that organizations such as colleges and universities prefer "diversity" because it is detached from struggles for equality throughout history, it is "a sign of lack of commitment to change," and it functions to "conceal the operation of systematic inequalities under the banner of difference" (p. 236). Similarly, Adams and Zúñiga (2018) echo that diversity approaches to education do not "necessarily include issues of inequality as fundamental to the ways in which diversity is experienced," might be weaponized to justify inequalities and injustices, or is systematically associated with privileges and oppressions (p. 41). In contrast, social justice and equity keep the spotlight on the extent to which as well as the ways in which education challenges and/or reproduces injustices and inequities in society. Generally, equity can be understood as "a standard for judging whether a state of affairs is just or unjust," fair or unfair, and caring or uncaring (Dowd & Bensimon, p. 9). Stewart (2018) advocates that approaches based in equity and justice, as opposed to those rooted in compositional diversity and inclusion, are more likely to lead to structural changes and revisions. As a political project, we argue that social justice and equity should be central to intercultural communication pedagogy and, as Alexander, Arasaratnam, Durham et al. (2014) note, deserve to be developed further concretely, specifically, and contextually.

We approach *culture* broadly and inclusively to include not just dominant social categories like race, class, gender, sexuality, nationality, and ethnicity, but also less salient intersecting identities such as ability, religion, immigration status, political affiliation, regionality, age, and more. Intercultural communication is the study of communication and representations of/with/about cultural groups and identifications. Our research with twenty intercultural communication instructors across the United States has identified diverse approaches to, lenses on, and conceptualizations of "cultures" to be one of the three core strengths of intercultural communication studies (Lawless & Chen, 2020). "Inter" could mean and take on various meanings. For some intercultural communication scholars, "inter" keeps the focus on interactions between individuals and/or groups from more different than similar cultural backgrounds. For other intercultural communication scholars, "inter" represents the space in-between paradigms to reimagine interparadigmatic expansions of the field (Halualani & Nakayama, 2010).

While there are other books that provide a variety of activities and theoretical foundations for engaging in this work (e.g., Adams, Bell, Goodman, & Joshi, 2016; Stringer & Cassiday, 2009), (critical) intercultural communication scholarship is uniquely positioned to contribute to conversations about teaching social justice. Even though (critical) intercultural communication scholars are not the only ones within the communication discipline interested and committed to social justice, intercultural communication approaches uniquely bring together focuses on communication, culture, and social justice. Here, we centralize human communication as inherently cultural practices (i.e., between teachers and students, among students, and external to the classroom) in an understanding of social justice.

The current political climate has brought a chill to the classroom especially around topics of xenophobia, racism, sexism, and other "sensitive" topics and issues that many of us thought we had made progress in the previous years and decades. (Critical) Intercultural communication scholarship offers new tools to restock the inventory. At the same time, the study of intercultural communication is interdisciplinary in nature and the context of pedagogy offers rich opportunities to consider its relevance across disciplines. We outline the difficult political contexts in which teaching for diversity and social justice takes place. As intercultural communication teacher-scholars, we write this book in that spirit to restock, retool, and reenergize how we teach for social justice at a particularly challenging, uncertain, and polarizing time.

INTERCULTURAL COMMUNICATION AND SOCIAL JUSTICE

Intercultural communication, at its core, encourages students and scholars to become curious and conscious about difference and how it affects everyday communication. The need for such consideration is indisputably growing amid public concern about what constitutes racism, political polemics about racial, religious, and national "Others," increasing attention to gender-based harassment, greater visibility of transgender communities, and dialogue about the constitutionality of ethnic studies, to name a few. Despite the great need for learning strategies for effective and appropriate intercultural communication, many educators remain timid and uncertain about what they should be discussing in class, what remains "too political" to discuss and take a stance on, and how to have nuanced conversations about such politically and emotionally charged topics. Indeed, many educators avoid these topics for fear of political retaliation or academic blacklisting.[1] We must have deliberate and intentional discussions about the pedagogy of intercultural communication *because* this subject has been targeted as something taboo. Intercultural communication pedagogy can lead to a charge of social justice for the next generation.

Our book builds upon traditional and critical approaches to intercultural communication in educational contexts. Most higher education institutions that offer classes in Communication (Studies) offer multiple sections of Intercultural Communication or Cross-Cultural Communication—Intercultural Communication has become one of the top three offerings in Communication Studies (in addition to Public Speaking and Interpersonal Communication). Whereas in the 1950s and 1960s Intercultural Communication was conceived of as a way to train members of the Foreign Service Institute (FSI) and other international wanderers, today's scholarship and course offerings expand the definition of culture beyond "nation-state" (Leeds-Hurwitz, 1990; Moon, 2010). Moreover, the study of Intercultural Communication education has shifted over the seven decades since the genesis of the field, withstanding harsh debates between social scientific and interpretive scholars, and later the "critical turn" (Denzin, 2010; Moon, 2010). As the field evolves, pedagogical approaches follow but have remained marginal in scholarly conversations and publications. While a growing number of scholars have defined a sub-field of *critical intercultural communication* and such work is more widely represented at regional and national communication conferences, an articulation of pedagogical approaches is slowly gaining traction.

Although intercultural communication scholarship has flourished over the past few decades, necessary conversations about *what* is—or should be—at the core of intercultural communication education and *how* to teach intercultural communication today remain limited. In the past decade, there has been a plethora of undergraduate textbooks and readers that have emerged for teaching intercultural communication in addition to what has already been in place. Just to name a few at random, in 2014, Baldwin, Coleman, González, and Shenoy-Packer published *Intercultural Communication for Everyday Life* with Wiley Blackwell. In 2015, Davis and Patterson-Masuka published *Intercultural Communication for Global Engagement* with Kendall Hunt. In 2016, Sorrells published the second edition of *Intercultural Communication: Globalization and Social Justice* with SAGE. The growing number of textbooks and readers reflects tremendous growth and diversification of the study of intercultural communication. At the same time, it also signals uneasiness about and/or challenges in teaching intercultural communication (e.g., Chen, 2014a; Chen, Simmons, & Kang, 2015). Paradoxically, producing more textbooks and readers is limited in directly addressing the pedagogical difficulties involved in teaching intercultural communication. Rather, there is a need for deliberate conversations and dialogues about *how* to teach intercultural communication and what is at the core of intercultural communication pedagogy(ies). Smith's (1982) seminal study, surveying content of intercultural communication courses at a time when "this field has graduated from an apprenticeship to a professional rank of scholarship and expertise" (p. 252), found that interpersonal adjustment, job skills, and cosmopolitanism were the three guiding principles for studying intercultural communication. Today, many U.S. colleges and universities position a course like Intercultural Communication as part of the generation education curricula fulfilling an aspect of some sort of diversity requirement. However, what is often missing is a discussion of diversity requirement *to what end* and *for whom*. Despite the strides the field has made, conversations about intercultural communication pedagogy remain sporadic. Building on the conversation that Atay and Toyosaki (2018) have started in their edited collection, *Critical Intercultural Communication Pedagogy*, this book continues to fill this gap by legitimizing intercultural communication pedagogy as a crucial tenet of the study of intercultural communication and fulfilling its pedagogical potentials to teach for social justice in challenging times.

Intercultural communication has both theoretical and pedagogical implications for other areas of the communication discipline and related disciplines. As such, we propose in this book a pedagogical integration of intercultural communication and critical communication pedagogy in teaching for social change. Our book facilitates an important dialogue around (re)thinking "difficult," "sensitive," or "challenging" classroom conversations related to intersecting cultural identity positions (e.g., racism, homophobia, and xenophobia). Specifically, intercultural, instructional, postcolonial, and public deliberation communication scholars have all written about engaging civil discourses around difficult conversations (with)in the communication classroom (e.g., Chen, 2014b; Cooks, 2001; Drabinski, 2011; Houston, 2004; Johnson & Bhatt, 2003; Meyer, 2007; Nagda, 2006; Rich & Cargile, 2004; Simpson, Causey, & Williams, 2007; Zompetti, 2006). We center these conversations within intercultural communication research, education, and praxis.

Facilitating discussions about diversities in the classroom is often accompanied by uncertainty, fear, and anxiety, among instructors and students for many, sometimes unknown, reasons (Goodman, 2010). These feelings can stem from conflicting ideologies (Hedley & Markowitz, 2001) or difficulty engaging students in theories and practices of social justice (Duffy, Mowatt, Fuchs, & Salisbury, 2014). In addition to these perspectives, we note that teaching topics related to difference is influenced by an instructor's standpoint and their institutional, departmental, and situational contexts. The lived experiences of the instructor and students within a class can significantly impact the types of topics that are discussed and the pedagogical approaches that are chosen. Demographics, paradigmatic, and philosophical assumptions about communication as a discipline, and training (or lack thereof) in critical and cultural issues are all important elements to consider. Additionally, some schools and departments readily incorporate topics such as race, gender, class, sexuality, disability, and so on into their curricula, while others find themselves more covertly incorporating these topics into course lectures and discussions. Finally, everyday, seemingly innocuous, factors such as the time of day that a class is offered, the time of year a class is taught, and the number of students in attendance can also influence the level of difficulty and/or success that comes with teaching certain topics. This book builds on intercultural communication and critical communication pedagogy to retool the pedagogical inventory of teaching for equity, inclusion, and social justice.

Those teachers who come before me inform the ways in which I approach this class/room. I never had a teacher who I idolized and tried to replicate; rather, I have taken lessons from those instructors who I learned the most content, those who were able to engage students in deep conversations, and those who had innovative practices for how to introduce and apply concepts. I had one undergraduate professor who was an authoritarian rhetorician. I learned more from his classes than any other instructor in my education. Though I am critical of his methods now, he was the single person I can point to who encouraged me to go to graduate school, made me feel "smart enough," and pushed me to read books that I thought were beyond my comprehension. His classes changed my perspective on external reality and my own. My teaching seeks to offer this level of empowerment to students who feel they lack knowledge and ability. In my MA level intercultural communication course, I had a teacher who was a "guide on the side." It was my first introduction to teaching that wasn't explicitly performative. And yet, I wanted her to step in and facilitate more when a white student said, "I identify as Black because all of my friends are Black." From her, I learned that there must be an intricate balance between asking questions, guiding responses, and challenging problematic understandings of content. In my doctoral program, I had a teacher who was committed to approaching the study of intercultural communication through a critical lens, and yet made sure we explored the history of the field and other paradigmatic approaches. From her, I took the need to focus on both depth and breadth and explaining the rationale for doing so. Teaching often requires us to step out of our comfort zone and be knowledgeable about a wide range of perspectives. Though I do not emulate a single instructor, I have grown into my own pedagogy—one that is inclusive but critical, engaging and not transmissive, empowering and challenging, and always reflexive.

Growing up in a system of education that is shaped and organized by Confucius's philosophy of approaching teaching as parenting（一日為師，終生為父）and valuing education as praxis in life, I am fortunate to have had many amazing teachers in my life. Having grown up celebrating annually Confucius's birthday as national teacher's day in Taiwan, I have developed a deep and profound respect for teachers and education as well as the classroom as a sacred space for learning. Also, I know that I would not have been where I am today without them. For instance, my fourth-grade teacher, Mr. Huang, was the first teacher who went out of his way to make sure that I and my classmates actually learned what we needed to learn to move on to the next grade. I recall my third grade being a year of changing substitute teachers who let my classmates and I off the hook not having to take learning seriously on and off for a full academic year. In contrast, I remember all the things that Mr. Huang had done inside and outside the classroom to show that he cared about all of his students (e.g., bringing us treats, spending time getting to know his students inside and outside the class). He made clear that not learning was not an option. My thesis advisor, Dr. Pratibha Shukla, was the first person who asked me where I would apply for my doctoral education—as opposed to if I would apply to a doctoral program. It is because of teachers/mentors like her that I ended up staying in U.S. academia. What makes these teachers memorable and special to me goes beyond how each of them conducted and taught their classes. They are great teachers to me because they are invested in me and my growth and because they embody and practice what they preach.

OVERVIEW OF CHAPTERS

A teacher does not have to be new to this course to consider revisiting their pedagogical commitments, nor do you have to be seasoned in order to understand the theoretical and pedagogical approaches we have laid out in each chapter. We invite you to take what works and leave the rest. In each chapter, we give a broad overview of a unit that might be covered in an Intercultural Communication course, including three to five key concepts and the theorists who developed them. Next, we describe the pedagogical challenges that may arise when teaching the unit. This is not an exhaustive list, but these challenges frequently arise in our own experience and, in some cases, were reported by respondents in research we conducted with instructors of Intercultural Communication. In response to such challenges, we offer several pedagogical activities that can help to navigate challenges and enhance the classroom conversations in each unit. We provide a list of potential discussion questions that might help students and teachers to better engage with the concepts. Activities might include published exercises from *Communication Teacher*, book club ideas, assignments, TED Talks, and/or podcasts. Finally, we offer stories from the field—narratives from leading scholars in the field about overcoming obstacles and navigating the terrain of intercultural communication—these stories were shared with us in our qualitative interviews.

Chapter 1: Articulating Philosophies and Assumptions

Here, we reflect on the approaches used to study/teach intercultural communication and the (re)framing needed to approach the subject. Each intercultural communication textbook will present the field through a different philosophical or paradigmatic lens. Our research shows that it is more useful to help students understand various approaches to intercultural communication and then work through a primary frame. This chapter articulates ways in which we can approach the discussion of paradigms (social scientific, interpretive, critical, feminist, queer, and postcolonial) and still take a social justice approach to the class.

Chapter 2: Communicating Power and Privilege

In teaching/learning for social justice, critical reflexivity about one's and others' identities paves the way for better communication about varying levels of power and privilege across differences that matter personally, socially, and historically. Chapter 2 examines issues, processes, and forces that affect how power, privilege, and difference are communicated to support, maintain, and/ or resist the status quo (e.g., whiteness, patriarchy, and neoliberalism). We describe and discuss communication tools for exposing existing power relations and making invisible privilege visible.

Chapter 3: Negotiating Avowed and Ascribed Identities for Social Justice

Critical reflection of the self and others in cultural terms is one foundation of intercultural communication education. In chapter 3, we review key scholarly works on identity, culture, and communication (e.g., Cultural Identity/Identification Theory, and intersectionality) with a particular focus on how avowed and ascribed identities are negotiated across contexts for social justice. Specifically, we describe both challenges and opportunities in negotiating intersecting identities for social justice inside and outside the classroom (e.g., race, gender, nationality, class, sexuality, ability, and immigration status). We also offer tools for processing identity avowals and ascriptions.

Chapter 4: Building Alliances

Chapter 4 explores the growing literature around intercultural alliances. Extending Collier's (1998) articulation of the concept, which includes (1) shared understanding of power and privilege, (2) recognition of history, and (3) an orientation of affirmation, this chapter develops upon previous chapters by articulating what relationships can look like within a social justice framework. Within this framework, we also describe approaches to teaching about microaggressions and engaging in consciousness of our everyday, taken-for-granted communication.

Chapter 5: Community Engagement for Social Justice

Our greater awareness of ourselves and others is enacted on a larger social level, in which we consider policies, social movements, and larger peace processes. Community building is an essential and indispensable aspect of teaching/learning for social justice. Striving for justice for all is a communal effort that requires buy-ins, dedications, and commitments from everyone. Chapter 5 reviews and describes ways, processes, and approaches for building a community for justice that honors diverse voices, communicates in power-with manners, and affirms humanity in a deeply divisive climate.

Chapter 6: Deconstructing Ideologies

Whereas chapter 4 explores communication on a micro-level (between people), this chapter moves to a macro-level to understand broader social discourses that exist outside of the individual yet influence our everyday communication. This chapter offers tools for teaching about ideology and hegemony, offering specific examples such as color blindness, ethnocentrism, and meritocracy.

Chapter 7: Thinking and Acting Globally

Teaching/learning for social justice is inherently a global project. The increasing forces, conditions, and processes of globalization today mandate a need to think and act both locally and globally. Chapter 7 reviews literature on cultural dimensions of globalization and enacting intercultural praxis as global citizenship. Grounded in this body of literature, we will discuss teaching/learning tools and activities that promote intercultural citizenship.

Chapter 8: "Assessing" Intercultural Pedagogies for Social Justice

An intercultural communication approach to teaching for social justice rests on pedagogical practices of critical reflexivity, ethnorelativism, praxis, and critical compassion for all. Chapter 8 ends with discussions and reflections about re-orienting academic "assessment" to match critical commitments of intercultural pedagogies and promote teaching/learning practices that are accountable to those commitments (e.g., identifying process-based learning outcomes and developing sensing/thinking/feeling learning outcomes).

Conclusions and Reflections: Teaching Social Justice in a Changing and Challenging Moment

In addition to the specific content we teach in Intercultural Communication, we must reflect on the ways in which we *experience* teaching these topics. In conclusion to the book we reflect on cultural battle fatigue, emotional labor, and the need for mentorship. We offer helpful suggestions for dealing with the pedagogical difficulties that arise in the teaching of diversity for social justice.

Appendix: Critical Intercultural Communication Activities

At the end of our book, you can find relevant activities and handouts that will make teaching these concepts a bit easier. Use these in conjunction with the units we have outlined or in new ways that engage difficult conversations in the classroom.

Social justice is inherent in this work, as described in each of the chapters. In discussing paradigmatic approaches, we are orienting students toward the possibility of social change as a goal for how we conduct research and learn about the world. By introducing the concept of *identities*, we open up the possibility of naming oppression and *who* has access to resources. Following discussions of power and privilege helps students to understand how power is imbalanced, tipping access to resources in inequitable directions. Learning about alliances ensures that our students have a shared goal of social change, an orientation that promotes learning about individual inequities and historical power imbalances. In teaching tools to identify and deconstruct ideologies, students are better able to challenge structures that reinforce power for privileged groups. Discussions of globalization make visible larger systems (e.g., international policies and practices) that block access to resources for oppressed groups, ensuring the rich get richer on a global scale. Community engagement provides tangible opportunities for students to participate in activism for social change within their own communities, where they can begin to understand the inequitable distribution of and access to resources on a local level. Finally, critical assessment of learning outcomes in the Intercultural Communication classroom creates an opportunity for educators to build learning outcomes that are driven by social change and understandings of inequity. We, as educators, may not think that the work we do has a tangible outcome when working toward social justice, but these topics create knowledge, build understanding, and present opportunities that are important in social justice work.

WHO IS THE AUDIENCE FOR THIS BOOK?

We wrote this book with several audiences in mind: (a) new instructors and graduate students; (b) instructors who have taught Intercultural Communication before and find it challenging; (c) those in charge of programmatic curriculum development and assessment.

New instructors and graduate students: This book will be useful in conjunction with instructional training in any communication program. This is a companion text that will supplement major Intercultural Communication textbooks and aid in first-time course development for new instructors. Communication programs that offer graduate seminars in pedagogy and instruction may find this text useful for engaging students in the challenges of teaching in the communication discipline. New instructors will get a foray into the myriad challenges of teaching the course and a strong grasp on how to navigate such obstacles. This book is especially useful for instructors who may have taught Public Speaking or Introduction to Communication and are taking a leap into teaching the Intercultural Communication course—a unique class that requires shifts in pedagogical approach.

Seasoned instructors of Intercultural Communication: In our research and in conversations with peers across the globe, we commonly hear that Intercultural Communication is a challenging course to teach because the subject is dynamic, politically charged, and complex. For this reason, instructors who have taught this course before may still find this book valuable. The chapters may introduce you to new concepts worthy of inclusion in syllabus updates and may offer tools for navigating discussions that you have found to be complicated and emotionally draining. Even if you have been teaching this course for years, you might come home after class and think, "How could I have done this better?" This book, then, is for you. Read and become reinvigorated about how you can work toward social justice in your classroom.

Curriculum development and assessment. As programs grow and change, it is important to revisit specific courses and their place in an ever-changing world. For those programs that are re-examining and re-aligning curriculum, this book is useful in developing new Intercultural Communication courses from inception to assessment. The tools in this book will help you identify student learning outcomes, assignments to assess those outcomes, and strategies for instructional delivery.

Whatever your position or role, use this book to address your personal and programmatic needs. It is our hope that this book expands your repertoire of responses to challenges and obstacles in the Intercultural Communication classroom, while also offering new insights into how the course can be taught.

My most memorable moments in the Intercultural Communication classroom are those in which students have an "aha!" moment! They feel some level of empathy from experiencing a simulation on poverty or meritocracy; they see examples of white privilege that make them consider their unearned advantage; they start to question history and context after viewing a documentary about U.S. foreign policy and its influence on immigration; they exhibit vulnerability in a community circle and come out as someone new. The Intercultural Communication classroom has the potential to fundamentally change the lens through which we view the world. It is also fraught with challenges and has left me feeling empty and aching on some days. When I first started teaching this course in 2010, I would wake up early from anxiety, thinking about how I would introduce the idea of structural racism, for example. I slowly needed to build a repertoire of responses to racist, sexist, or homophobic comments that would enter the classroom in some seemingly innocuous fashion. "I don't think we should give the Japanese reparations because they DID attack Pearl Harbor. What were we supposed to do?" "I don't have white privilege because I sunburn easily." "I would never get in a cab with a Black driver. I don't want to get stabbed!" I want to say the right thing to help students deconstruct these ideas for themselves AND make sure that I am attending to those students who could be hurt by what their peers just said. I have a deep responsibility to do many things at once if I want the transformative potential of this course to take hold. It is a lot to shoulder, but there is a huge impact.

As an Intercultural Communication educator since 2008, my memorable moments about teaching this course have been times either when students (and I) left the class feeling hurt, unheard, and alienated or when students (and I) left the class feeling supported, validated, and heard, particularly around contentious and challenging issues such as racism, sexism, and homophobia. Last week, I received an email from a self-identified Latina student after having led a conversation about colonialism in class. For the first time in this sixty-person, hybrid class in which we only meet fifty minutes twice a week, more students spoke up, but mostly white male students. The student emailed me about how frustrated and angry she felt regarding the conversation we just had in class; she wrote: "While I know everyone is entitled to their own opinion, and once again I am not very informed of any of the historical references brought up in class today. I got very frustrated listening to some examples some of my classmates shared today. While I do not know the whole context of how they were talking about them but for example, someone said something about colonialism and he made it seem like it was a good thing, and another one gave an example of a book he had read about internment camps also being a 'good thing.' I also noticed they were white men." I emailed the student right away, and I wrote: "I see that it is frustrating to witness when negative impacts of slavery and colonialism are downplayed. I should have named the downplaying. Thank you for bringing this to my attention. Absolutely, the positions of the speakers definitely matter. I am not sure if I heard that it was suggested that colonialism and internment camps were 'good.' Both are complicated issues. I am with you that it is hard for me to understand how there can be positives associated with both. In the moment, I did note that more men were speaking up as you did. I will work on facilitating and encouraging more less-heard voices." The student actually came into my office that afternoon and talked for half an hour. I will be using this incident in class the following week when we meet again. There have been many memorable incidents like this in my Intercultural Communication classroom. They are loaded, tricky, and complicated. At the same time, growing in my ability to facilitate those moments is what makes this class meaningful to me.

We envision an Intercultural Communication classroom where students bring all their lived experiences, struggles, cultural wealth, and individual lenses to bear on the content. We strive for all members of the class to be empowered through learning, to embrace discomfort when growing, and to feel safe in sharing. Students should have the tools to think critically and actively engage in communities. There should be a community of trust in which everyone listens as deeply as possible while recognizing their varying levels of privileges and oppressions within context(s). We want to reimagine the teacher-student relationship and move away from a top-down hierarchy that frames the teacher as all-knowing, the students as empty vessels waiting to be filled with knowledge, and communication as transmissive. These relationships are built on vulnerability, honesty, deep reflection, and compassion. An inclusive community built on these pedagogies does not value "all opinions as equal," but rather, collectively speaks back against ideologies that are deemed harmful (e.g., white supremacy). We hope that this book accomplishes these goals.

Chapter 1

Articulating Philosophies and Assumptions

Although the turn to deconstructive and post-structuralist theorizing . . . offered many exciting theoretical possibilities for the discipline, I began to notice a curious phenomenon: the new paradigm's rapid hegemonization in many circles of scholarship.

(Mendoza, 2010, p. 99)

Indeed, linkages among the postpositivist, interpretive, and critical approaches can magnify great insight on culture and intercultural communication especially in terms of multilayered contexts that involve privatized experience, perception, and behavior and larger structures, conditions, and histories. But we must also ask ourselves about the areas in which these approaches depart and collide.

(Halualani & Nakayama, 2010, pp. 10–11)

In this chapter, we reflect on the approaches used to study/teach intercultural communication and the (re)framing needed to approach the subject. Each intercultural communication textbook will present the field through a specific stance on philosophical or paradigmatic lens even though the particular stance might not be identified, named, or explained. Our research shows that it is pedagogically useful to help students understand various approaches to intercultural communication and then work through a primary frame (Lawless & Chen, 2020). This chapter articulates ways in which we can approach the discussion of paradigms (e.g., social scientific, interpretive, critical, feminist, queer, and postcolonial) and still take a social justice approach to the class.

BACKGROUND

Paradigms, or lenses through which we view the world, shape and inform our understanding of culture, communication, and the relationship between the two. A paradigmatic approach can also influence how one defines these constructs. Paradigmatic differences in the field are both a strength and a struggle in our ongoing effort to define the landscape of intercultural communication as a field and as a pedagogy (Lawless & Chen, 2020). A discussion of paradigms, philosophical assumptions, and research goals is important in any level of intercultural communication education because it "creates a pedagogical opportunity for students to both see culture through different vantage points (rather than be handed a simple definition from which to base assumptions), and advance their critical sensibilities through a trajectory of culture that continually shifts over time and across cultures" (Lawless & Chen, 2020, p. 6). When we ask our students on the first day of class, "What is culture or are cultures?" they likely have a hyper-simplified definition in mind and expect us to detail our own singular definition for culture. Imagine their discomfort and confusion when we offer five or more definitions of "culture" while making a move to stress cultures as plural and dynamic:

- Culture is a set of shared practices, language, beliefs, and values.
- Culture is dominant or hegemonic practices in a society.
- Culture is shifting tensions between what is shared and unshared.
- Culture is a contested zone.
- Culture is a critical dance with difference (Collier, 2014).

If we were to look at this (brief) list as a student who is new to the study of cultures and/or critical inquiry, we might play it safe and choose the first definition. The subsequent definitions require a development of the critical sensibilities noted before. In our classrooms, we encourage students to be open to "not taking the easy definition" and moving toward what is messy, nuanced, and complex. This is what entire semesters together are for.

Depending on the textbook you choose, different paradigmatic approaches to the study of intercultural communication are foregrounded. Some textbooks choose to highlight multiple paradigmatic approaches as a means of surveying the field more broadly. For example, Martin and Nakayama (2018) describe social scientific, interpretive, and critical approaches to the study of culture and communication, followed by an articulation of a *dialectical* approach that allows readers to move across paradigms to understand cultures. In their theorization outside of their widely used textbook, Martin and Nakayama (1999) identify four primary paradigms for the study of culture and communication: functionalist/postpositivist/social scientific, interpretive,

Table 1.1. Paradigmatic Approaches to the Study of Intercultural Communication

Functionalist/ Postpostivist/ Social Scientific Approach	Interpretive Approach	Critical Humanist Approach	Critical Structuralist Approach
• Views culture as a variable, often as a nation-state • Cultures have predictable characteristics upon which we can draw conclusions • Culture (or membership in a cultural group) determines communication	• Culture is socially constructed and emergent • Culture is something that can be observed and understood • Culture influences communication and communication influences culture	• Culture is socially constructed • Human consciousness is informed by larger social ideologies • Communication reinforces cultural ideologies but can also be used to resist and create change	• Culture is societal structures • Dominant structures enable and constrain intercultural communication • Communication reinforces social structures (culture) and can also be used to resist and create change

Adapted from Martin & Nakayama (2010)

critical humanist, and critical structuralist. This more nuanced discussion of paradigmatic approaches accounts for postcolonial lenses, and other divergences in an otherwise monolithic critical approach. Each approach offers different definitions of culture and communication (see table 1.1).

Though not exhaustive, this review of paradigms highlights a broad survey of the primary approaches to the study of culture and communication. An overview of multiple paradigms allows students from a variety of standpoints to enter into intercultural communication with a goal and a foundational framework for how they might conceptualize culture. For example, a biology major might initially connect with a functionalist understanding of culture, having been trained with the scientific method and the goal of objectivity. An anthropology major might be more interested in approaching culture through an interpretive lens, likely having been exposed to ethnographic methodologies. Political science majors might find themselves interested in how they can create policies that will influence the material consequences of marginalized cultural groups, aligning more with a critical humanist or critical structuralist approach. Indeed, in our research about the strengths and weaknesses of Intercultural Communication pedagogy, we found that many new and veteran instructors of this course were drawn to the social scientific aspects of the field, sometimes making a later arc toward critical and/or interpretive paradigms (Lawless & Chen, 2020). In surveying the paradigmatic approaches, instructors are also able to highlight the sheer depth of the discipline. Surveying paradigms in the Intercultural Communication course helps to "articulate an identifiable history in the field that is easy to convey to students who are new to conceptualizations of culture through a communication lens" (Lawless & Chen, 2020, p. 4).

Interparadigmatic Approaches

We often tell our students that, although it may be easy to choose one approach and maintain a singular conception of communication and culture throughout their studies, there is much to be borrowed/learned from other approaches. Also, we can *all* share the goal of social justice, regardless of our paradigmatic alignments. Furthermore, mirroring the in-between spaces in which intercultural communication often lives, we argue that interparadigmatic approaches and lenses enrich appreciations for the study, inquiry, and praxis of intercultural communication.

On thinking through bridging paradigms, Mendoza (2010) reminds us that "to bridge is to straddle worlds—whether by choice or by force—and to be compelled to find a way of connecting the two in ways that make sense" (p. 100). On their recent review of intercultural inquiry, Martin and Nakayama (2010) revealed an increased blurring of the lines between paradigms, making it important to understand the assumptions of multiple paradigmatic approaches. When we offer a reason to explore beyond what students may already be comfortable with, we also create a rationale for the movement toward critical approaches. There are several ways into interparadigmatic conceptualizations of culture. Martin and Nakayama (2010) note four: liberal pluralism, interparadigmatic borrowing, multiparadigmatic collaboration, and dialectic perspective. Liberal pluralism honors what each paradigm can bring to specific topics of study, while interparadigmatic borrowers being to integrate multiple paradigmatic goals (e.g., understanding *and* social change). Multiparadigmatic collaborations draw upon the expertise of multiple researchers, whereas the dialectic perspective invites researchers/students to imagine culture and communication as fluid, complex, and changing, requiring our approach to study such concepts be equally dynamic.

Collier (2014) provides several examples of the integration of multiple paradigms in what she calls critical/interpretive (or critical-interpretive) approaches to the study of intercultural communication. As she explains, the "/" between two distinctive paradigms allows her to approach the critical and interpretive perspectives as "informing each other and interdependent" while privileging the critical perspective (p. 7). Collier's work has offered guidance to those qualitative researchers who have long felt the need to move beyond ethnographic understanding, toward social and structural change, without being tied to either ethnography or textual analysis. Similarly, Covarrubias (2008) demonstrates combining interpretive (ethnography of communication) and critical approaches (whiteness studies) to explore how Native American students become marginalized through discursive strategies in college settings. Specifically, she identifies a pattern of masked silence sequences in which discriminatory silences follow hurtful comments against students from minoritized groups and thus function to (re)produce discrimination against students based on their minoritized group membership such as race. Drawing on both the phenomenology of speaking and critical autoethnography, Sekimoto and Brown (2016) narrate their experiences of speaking in racialized tongue as "habituated embodiment, resulting from an orchestration of vocal, auditory, and sensorimotor experiences within a particular system of cultural and ideological practice" (p. 102). Together, scholarship of integrated and/or integrating multiple paradigms evidences a need to better understand complex and at times contested intercultural communication phenomena through interparadigmatic approaches.

Paradigm Purism?

Some might challenge the notion that there are strengths in surveying the breadth of approaches to studying intercultural communication. We are still at a critical juncture in the field, battling for importance, credibility, and recognition, if not relevance. Qualitative methods, in general, only recently became more widely accepted in the field of communication studies. Denzin (2010) notes in his *Qualitative Manifesto* an emergence of "paradigm purists" or those who believe "postpositivism and other 'isms' cannot be combined because of the differences between their underlying paradigm assumptions" (p. 21). Indeed, it can be difficult to justify a simultaneous commitment to objectivity and subjectivity, for example. Paradigm purism led to steadfast commitments and an onslaught of paradigmatic and methodological criticism. We believe that while there is room for paradigm preference, such staunch approaches to the instruction of (intercultural) communication leads to positions that frame research about communication phenomena as either scientific or armchair inquiry, high quality or low quality, truth or opinion. These binary criticisms limit our scope and audience. The continuation of the paradigm wars from the 1970s and 1980s is woefully unsuccessful in the integration and continuation of intercultural communication as a field of study. Indeed, Mendoza (2010) reminds us of the hypocrisy of "theoretical hegemony" as a way to police communication and limit dissenting opinions (p. 99). She urges us to "not throw out the baby of collective representation with the functionalist bathwater" (p. 98). Instead, "educators can bolster the field [of intercultural communication] by carrying their own paradigmatic commitments and still give credence to the field as a whole" which honors our history of the field, highlights its strengths, and embraces an intellectual community of scholars rather than further fragmenting the field (Lawless & Chen, 2020, p. 14). You can ask yourself several questions to help guide your decisions about course content (Table 1.2).

Choosing What to Cover

Table 1.2. Tool for Determining Course Content

Ask Yourself...	Consider...	What Should I Cover?
What is my pedagogical goal?	Is it to offer breadth, depth, or both?	
What is my timeframe?	Do you have enough time in the semester to cover multiple approaches?	
	Are you teaching a truncated course?	
	Are you teaching a special topics course that requires you to be focused on a single approach?	
What are your institutional goals/mission(s)?	Does your institution promote social justice in its mission?	
	Is your program more theory driven or applied?	
What are you comfortable with?	What is your background?	
	What are you willing to learn?	
	How comfortable are you with being challenged?	
What direction is the field/new research headed?	What current issues warrant study?	
	How can we address new developments?	
What institutional contexts do you face?	What population of students do you work with?	
	What limitations are placed on your pedagogies?	
	Are you required to use a specific textbook?	
What textbook/materials have you chosen?	Does the text introduce multiple approaches?	
	Can you supplement with readings that introduce multiple approaches?	

An interparadigmatic approach can be useful for bringing multiple voices to the table, while still introducing a goal of social justice. After all, if we can begin to deepen our understanding of differences and work toward *understanding* positionalities, then we can better grasp how inequities arise and are perpetuated. Encourage students to brainstorm how each of the paradigms can work toward a shared goal of justice and equity.

KEY CHALLENGES

We have laid out an argument for surveying multiple paradigms as a starting point for intercultural communication inquiry. This approach is not without challenges. Primarily, we are limited by our own experiences, knowledges, and expertise. It is admittedly easier to teach from a paradigm that we espouse. We are more passionate about those approaches to inquiry that we align with and we can demonstrate our commitment to particular philosophical assumptions in an unwavering manner. Even so, we are asking students to become comfortable with discomfort and we must first meet this challenge ourselves. Taking this approach can help us to fill in our own knowledge gaps and strengthen the foundation of our own commitments. Moreover, we can serve as exemplars for students who question why a survey of approaches to intercultural communication inquiry is important.

Time may be a more pressing constraint. You might be asking, "How do I cover so much information in a fifteen- or sixteen-week semester?" What we advocate for here is not a fully developed investigation of all definitions, assumptions, and paradigms. Rather, an introduction to multiple modes of inquiry and a subsequent rationale of why you choose to focus on one (perhaps a messier definition and vantage point) simplifies a discussion of the history and trajectory of the field. Students should be prepared to critique (or at least understand critiques of) outdated or monolithic conceptions of culture in a modern world. Simply put, you do not need to give full attention to all paradigms (even we have not presented an exhaustive list). However, you should consider introducing the notion that there is not a singular conception of culture and why that matters.

The discussion of paradigms in and of itself reproduces boundaries for the ways we can/should study culture. For example, approaches to Afrocentricity or Asiacentricity often live in the periphery of the field, reproducing Western/Eurocentric notions of cultures and interculturality. Including additional readings about these modes of inquiry can help us to introduce the notion that Western-centered epistemologies should be challenged.

STORIES FROM THE FIELD

Lindsay Scott, Lone Star College

Paradigms extend beyond how we study culture and communication, but also how we approach our teaching, the assumptions we make about the world around us, as well as the lens in which we interpret scholarship. The classroom is a battleground for these paradigms to emerge and sometimes collide. Although our students might not have the vocabulary to name paradigms, they arrive with one. As a critical/interpretive scholar, I find myself more comfortable facilitating discussions and sharing research that closely aligns with philosophical assumptions. At the same time, I recognize the value that each paradigm brings to our field, and I have a commitment to sharing that with my students.

In my community college classroom, I approach my course as an opportunity to build a strong foundation for the study of communication. In this space, students are best served if they understand the basics about paradigms. I introduce paradigms as different approaches to problem-solving. I explain to students that the paradigmatic approach depends on the question(s) that we are seeking answers and the problem(s) that we are trying to solve. When students understand that each paradigm is a tool, and they can identify the particular use for that tool, then they are better prepared to interpret research and articulate their own paradigm. Students also see that as our problems become more complex and the answers that we seek more nuanced, our tools must become more sophisticated. To demonstrate this, we plot the social scientific, interpretive, critical, feminist, queer, and postcolonial paradigms on a graph to show how the field has responded to different sociopolitical contexts. Conversations about paradigms are complex, but do not need to be overwhelming. I have found that when I meet students where they are, I am more likely to take them to where they need to be.

Dr. Scott points to a challenge with the study of paradigmatic approaches—the topic seems overwhelming and cursory to the study of culture. However, her story sheds light on the importance and impact of these conversations, reminding us that foundational legwork is important inside the intercultural communication classroom and as a tool for more holistic understandings of the world.

PEDAGOGICAL ACTIVITIES

Understanding Paradigms in Intercultural Communication Research

After discussing various approaches to intercultural communication research (e.g., social scientific, interpretive, critical, postcolonial, feminist), students navigate their college/university databases to find research within the field that utilizes each of the paradigms. After finding a suitable article, students annotate the article, pointing out reasons *why* the article operates from a particular paradigm. Alternatively, the instructor can select articles ahead of time, asking students to scan each article and determine which paradigm builds the foundation for each article.

Just Another Brick in the Wall ... or Not? A Paradigm Introduction Activity

In this published activity (see Kelly & Davis, 2011), students are asked to scientifically study a wall. Later, they are asked to describe the unique reality of the wall, leading to their contemplation of the best paradigms to understand and study human communication. The author includes appropriate extensions for the critical paradigm and discussion questions that help to expose and challenge philosophical assumptions.

Teaching Metatheory through Research Application and Design

In this published example of an exercise for graduate students (see Miller & Wieland, 2019), students are encouraged to compare paradigms, engage with philosophical differences, and develop strategies to challenge paradigms and assumptions outside of their preferred commitments. Instructors assign one article to all graduate students in the class. Students are later put into small groups and assigned a different paradigm. Each group must (re)design the assigned study using the paradigm they were given. In doing so, they are asked to detail how assumptions, rationale, biases, and other considerations inform the theory and research.

Unpacking Paradigms through the Language of Diversity and Inclusion to Equity and Justice

In an essay published in Inside Higher Ed, a media company and online publication that provides news, opinion, resources, events, and jobs focused on college and university topics, Stewart (2017) argues for replacing diversity and inclusion rhetoric (a.k.a. "language of appeasement") with language that promotes equity and justice to instigate institutional change: https://www.insidehighered.com/views/2017/03/30/colleges-need-language-shift-not-one-you-think-essay. In a way, the differing language here reflects underlying worldviews about "diversity" across paradigms. Engage students in mapping the paradigms onto the differing language in table 1.1 and fill in the missing language for the interpretive paradigm.

VIDEOS AS TEACHING TOOLS: THE DANGER OF A SINGLE STORY—CHIMAMANDA ADICHIE (2009)

Adichie's (2009) TED talk highlights a need for multiplicity in an increasingly complex world today. She warns against the danger of hearing a singular story about another person, country, or culture, which runs the risk of critical misunderstandings. Instead, Adichie advocates multiple and overlapping stories. When viewing paradigms as stories, this TED talk can be used to engage students in thinking about the pros and cons of using one or multiple paradigms in studying intercultural communication.

DISCUSSION QUESTIONS

1. Why/how do paradigms matter for an understanding of intercultural communication?
2. How does each paradigm frame the way we think/communicate about culture?
3. Which paradigm do you feel you most align with? Why?
4. Can somebody be aligned with more than one paradigm? Why/why not?
5. What paradigm do you think I (the instructor) most align with? Why?
6. How do you see paradigms operating in your daily life?
7. When working with somebody who operates from a different paradigm, what should we be mindful of?

Chapter 2

Communicating Power and Privilege

How do you begin to engage power when the stakes involve the larger goals of liberation, justice, voice and the power to name, the dismantling of legacies of colonialist oppression, and a culture's self-determination?

(Halualani & Nakayama, 2010, p. 4)

Close attention to the webs of power we weave and into which we are woven renders visible the affective labor we invest into the lives of others, and how that labor is constitutive of the selves we are becoming.

(Carrillo Rowe, 2008, p. 177)

Power sustains privilege in vivid and tragic ways to the extent that marginalized group members are uninvited to participate in what the academy represents unless they forfeit their desire to have their identities affirmed by the academy via institutionalized practices and/or curricular reform.

(Hendrix, Jackson, & Warren, 2003, p. 183)

Keeping in mind that how power and privilege are communicated (or not) matters for teaching and learning, in this chapter, we first summarize four conceptions of power that are most relevant and/or commonly referenced by intercultural communication scholars. We then synthesize three sets of key characteristics of privilege as they relate to power and communication, which is followed by discussions of key challenges, a story from the field by Dr. Anjana Mudambi, and pedagogical activities. Rather than addressing power and privilege as they come up in classroom interactions, we recommend proactively and preemptively engaging with students in intentional and deliberative conversations about how power and privilege might play out early on.

BACKGROUND

The classroom is a power-laden space with racialized/gendered/classed/sexualized cultural expectations, norms, and practices that work to sustain patterns of systemic privileging of some bodies over others. How intersecting cultural identities are communicated, represented, negotiated, and/or resisted across intercultural communication contexts always already involve unequal power relations and differential privileges—whether or not one is aware of their presence and influence. To critically reflect on one's own and others' cultural identity positions, in a sense, is to willingly interrogate, with both honesty and heart, how power and privilege emerge, circulate, and work to benefit some over others. That is, power and privilege orchestrate and organize how different identities are located, experienced, talked about, enacted, and/or performed in particular and specific ways that can support, maintain, and/or resist the status quo. This chapter considers how we can challenge ourselves and one another to become more aware of the ways in which asymmetries of power and privilege are deeply entrenched in our everyday thinking, living, and acting. For instance, this could mean becoming aware of how a "well-intentioned" and ethical person is also capable of participating in (re)producing social injustice whether knowingly or unknowingly.

Foregrounding power and privilege is one of the defining concerns, principles, and/or pillars of critical intercultural communication studies (e.g., Collier, 2002; Halualani, Mendoza, & Drzewiecka, 2009; Halualani & Nakayama, 2010). Early on, the centralizing of power relations, structures, and ideologies instigated re-theorization of culture as sites of (power) struggles and contested zones. Over time, the foregrounding of power relations, structures, and ideologies has also opened many doors for intercultural communication research, pedagogy, and activism. In the pedagogical arena, Atay and Toyosaki (2018) articulate the goal of critical intercultural communication pedagogy as aiming "to understand, critique, transform, and intervene upon the dynamics of power and domination embedded inside and outside classroom walls through careful, complex, nuanced, and intersectional analyses of education practices and our identities" (p. ix). How we attend to power and privilege vis-à-vis communication matters.

UNPACKING AND COMMUNICATING POWER

What does "power" mean to you? How do you define this complex concept? French and Raven (1959) describe the processes of power as "pervasive, complex, and often disguised" in society (p. 150). Intercultural communication scholars interested in social justice would agree that power matters and communication plays a critical role in how power comes to matter (e.g., Allen, 2011). In general, power is a complex and multidimensional construct that takes on and can be exercised and (re)produced in various forms such as a position that one occupies, an ability to control and/or dominate others, as a process of social influence, and more.

Based on your conceptualization of power, how do you understand and approach the relationship between power and (intercultural) communication? Generally, communication and power become interlinked in dynamic ways. Allen (2011) unpacks how we as social actors enact (unequal and asymmetrical) power relations through communication. Specifically, Allen (2011) identifies language use, everyday talk, and physical appearance as key processes and sites in which power relations are enacted vis-à-vis communication. We have summarized in the following text conceptions of power that are most relevant and/or commonly referenced by intercultural communication scholars: (a) power as capital; (b) power as relational and social influence; and (c) power as "archeology of knowledge."

Power as Capital

French sociologist Pierre Bourdieu (1930–2002) conceptualizes power as capital in that he extends the idea of economic interests to include "symbolic" interests such as noneconomic goods, services, and resources. That is, Bourdieu extends and broadens "the language of economic interest and strategy to all areas of cultural and social life" (Swartz, 1997, p. 67) by conceptualizing social and cultural resources as capitals that function for individuals and groups to maintain their positions of power and status in society. In general, Bourdieu considers a wide array of resources as cultural capitals ranging from verbal facility to speak in a desirable way, to aesthetic preferences that can elevate one's social status, to educational credentials and more. Compared with economic capitals, cultural capitals are generally considered less stable and less universal. Specifically, Bourdieu analyzes three different states in which cultural capitals exist: (1) an embodied state, (2) an objectified state, and (3) an institutionalized state (Swartz, 1997). *Cultural capitals in the embodied state* refer to "the ensemble of cultivated dispositions that are internalized by the individual through socialization and that constitute schemes of appreciation and understanding" (Swartz, 1997, p. 76). Since early childhood, children are socialized to invest in, acquire, and appreciate group-based cultivated dispositions through consuming and accumulating cultural goods and services that are available such as music, books, and popular culture. Thus, the acquisition of cultivated dispositions can "translate original class-based inequities into cultural differences" (Swartz, 1997, p. 76) that distinguish one cultural group from another. *Cultural capitals in the objectified state* refer to objects such as books and instruments that require learned cultural abilities to use, consume, and/or apprehend. *Cultural capitals in the institutionalized form* means educational credential systems such as the higher education system. Together, cultural capitals in different states and forms increasingly become the new basis of social stratifications whether based on class, race, gender, and more.

Power as Relational and Social Influence

Power constitutes all relationships and emerges in relationships. People don't *have* power. Grounded in this orientation, French and Raven (1959) understand power as processes of social influence that constitute and emerge in workplace relationships to affect psychological change. Specifically, they have identified five bases of power that they deem mostly common and important in the workplace setting: reward power, coercive power, legitimate power, referent power, and expert power. *Reward power* refers to an ability to reward. *Coercive power* involves an ability to punish and "manipulate the attainment of valences" (French & Raven, 1959, p. 157). *Legitimate power*, the most complex of the five, stems from internalized values that person A has a legitimate right to influence person B and also that person B is obligated to accept such influence. *Referent power* addresses a form of identification with and reverence gained by someone with strong relational skills. *Expert power* refers to an attributed perception of knowledge, expertness, or specialized skillsets. As an example, challenging and complicating the Black/white racial binary, Mudambi (2015) deconstructs the discourse of "brownness" in the case of Arizona's SB 1070 as highly contextualized racial formation that is aligned with the construction of "illegal" immigrants based on shared struggles with discrimination among Latinx and South Asians. Her study highlights the relational and social "power of others to interpret and ascribe a brown person's identity" (p. 55).

Similarly, Carrillo Rowe (2008) considers how "the lines of intimacy, trust, and collaboration that we build with others are embedded in power" and connect to circuits of power (p. 1). Drawing on conversations with twenty-eight self-identified academic feminists as well as her own narratives, Carrillo Rowe examines feminist alliances as "a politics of relation" at the conjuncture between intimacy and institutional power. Contextualized within whiteness, heterosexism, and feminism, Carrillo Rowe attends to relational politics of feminist alliances and coalitions (such as differential belonging, betrayal, and innocence) across racial and other boundaries within academia. As the power lines of academia separate and prevent radical belonging and coalitional relationships between white feminists and feminists of color, Carrillo Rowe urges transracial feminist alliances "where 'power over' may be renamed as 'power with' and 'power to'" (2008, p. 1). This shift from a power-over to *power-with* relation is a core theme across the works of many intercultural communication scholars invested in social justice (e.g., Heuman, 2015).

Power as "Archaeology of Knowledge"

In *The Archaeology of Knowledge and the Discourse of Language*, Michel Foucault (1972) approaches archaeology as describing "discourses as practices specified in the element of the archive" that systematically governs what can be said, determines the appearance of statements/events/things, and defines how the statements/events/things occur and function (p. 131). This process of archeological description can also be known as analyzing discursive formation. In this view, power is productive in the sense that power is produced vis-à-vis discourses as practices obeying certain rules (Foucault, 1972, p. 138). When viewed as productive, power is not inherently positive or negative. Rather, power can produce negative and/or positive consequences and implications for individuals and cultural groups. Also, power is not located in the individual, nor the system. Rather, power governs the culturally and historically specific ways in which we live, we know, we speak, we think, we feel, and more.

Following a Foucauldian approach, Boler (1999) examines, in *Feeling Power: Emotions and Education*, dominant discourses of/about emotions as a site of power and resistance that "reflect linguistically-embedded cultural values and rules" across class, race, and gender (p. 6). She argues that emotions become a site of social control within education specifically as well as in the society generally. Individuals across class, race, and gender are not always explicitly controlled, forced, or coerced into feeling certain ways. More often than not, governed by dominant discourses, individuals willingly participate in, if not automatically consent to, producing expected emotions based on classed, raced, and gendered expectations.

Broadly speaking, intercultural communication scholars and teachers invested in social justice approach power as constitutive of communication and are committed to analyzing, interrogating, if not disrupting, power in its various forms, manifestations, circuits, and functions. Also, intercultural communication teacher-scholars are uniquely positioned to take culture-centered approaches to power and communication.

UNPACKING AND COMMUNICATING POWER AND PRIVILEGE

In your experiences, how does power relate to privilege? In a sense, power can become manifested as privilege and privilege may confer power. We have synthesized the following key characteristics of privilege as it relates to power and communication.

Privilege as Invisible and Unearned

First published in 1988, Peggy McIntosh's landmark essay, "White Privilege and Male Privilege: A Personal Account of Coming to See Correspondences through Work in Women's Studies," is arguably one of the most cited articles on whiteness and privilege. McIntosh, as a white woman faculty member in Women's Studies, was inspired to write this essay based on her parallel observations and critiques of her own "trouble facing white privilege" in juxtaposition to her experiences with "men's reluctance to acknowledge male privilege" (1997, p. 291). To illustrate the daily effects of white privilege in her life, McIntosh authors and details a list of forty-six specific ways in which she benefits from her skin color privilege such as #37 "I can be pretty sure of finding people who would be willing to talk with me and advise me about my next steps, professionally" (1997, p. 294), which she has continued to extend to include more. Speaking as a white woman, McIntosh describes "white privilege as an invisible package of unearned assets which I can count on cashing in each day, but about which I was 'meant' to remain oblivious. White privilege is like an invisible weightless knapsack of special provisions, assurances, tools, maps, guides, codebooks, passports, visas, clothes, compass, emergency gear, and blank checks" (1997, p. 291). McIntosh describes privilege as existing "when one group has something of value that is denied to others simply because of the groups they belong to, rather than because of anything they've done or failed to do" (as cited in Johnson, 2001, p. 23). Due to power hierarchies and circuits, those belonging to privileged groups experience privilege as invisible and elusive.

McIntosh (1997) distinguishes between two types of privilege: privilege as "conferred dominance" and privilege as "unearned entitlement." First, *conferred dominance* refers to occupying positions (such as based on race and/or gender) that enable one to systematically overpower another, grant one permission to control, or give one license to be thoughtless toward another. Second, an *unearned advantage and/or entitlement* that is afforded systematically has to do with an advantage or entitlement (such as a sense of belonging in society and having access to quality health care) that is restricted to some but not others. Since privilege is systematically afforded and thus unearned, an individual belonging to a privileged group cannot just give up the associated privilege. Thus, McIntosh concludes that "obliviousness about white advantage, like obliviousness about male advantage, is kept strongly enculturated in the United States so as to maintain the myth of meritocracy, the myth that democratic choice is equally available to all" (p. 298).

As complex as how privilege and power work together to (re)produce interlocking systems of domination, some of the specific ways in which McIntosh originally described benefiting from her skin color privilege have been critiqued to be more about her class privilege and less about her race privilege especially within education (e.g., Lensmire et al., 2013). As an example, Lensmire and colleagues (2013) state that "McIntosh's ideas of white privilege ignore issues of social class and geography and end up functioning as a sort of test or filter in which the only way to pass—as a good white person and good white teacher—is to acquiesce publicly to McIntosh's claims about how white privilege works" (p. 412). Rather than viewing such critiques as undermining McIntosh's benchmark contribution, we the authors believe that critiques like these are important and showcase pedagogical challenges involved in doing social-justice work within educational institutions. More importantly, the critiques signal *differential* challenges for white teachers and teachers of color committed to anti-racism and social-justice pedagogy.

Privilege as Paradox

Since privilege is defined and organized in relation to a group or social category (race, gender, sexuality, and nationality), Johnson (2001) argues that individuals can experience privilege paradoxically—"*being* privileged without *feeling* privileged" (emphasis in original, p. 36). As he puts it, "Race privilege is more about *white* people than it is about white *people*" (emphasis in original, Johnson, 2001, p. 34). Thus, it is possible for a self-identified white person to lose race privilege if people do not think or racialize the person as white. Further, belonging to a privileged category improves one's odds in favor of certain advantages, preferential treatments, and valued access; however, it does not guarantee anything. In particular, Johnson unpacks "the paradox that privilege doesn't necessarily make you happy" (2001, p. 38). Paradoxically, even though belonging to a privileged category does not guarantee anything such as happiness, the privilege still exists and matters in the social world. Another reason that privilege does not guarantee happiness is privilege can also "exact a cost from those who have it" (Johnson, 2001, p. 39). The cost might be struggling with the knowledge that the social systems dominate and take advantage of those belonging to the oppressed categories, feeling guilty about having unearned privilege, and more. Johnson's (2001) notion of privilege as paradox highlights the experiential and affective components of teaching and learning about privilege, which matters as much as cognitive understanding of how privilege works systematically.

Privilege as Intersectional

As social systems such as whiteness, patriarchy, and capitalism reinforce one another to uphold the status quo, privilege is inherently intersectional. Kimberlé Crenshaw (1991), a legal scholar, first conceived intersectionality to understand the interlocking systems of injustices and oppressions that structure the raced and gendered bodies. Intersectionality, rooted in Black feminist thought, has been developed out of a need to address and confront racism/classism/heterosexism within and across feminist movements (Collins, 2000; Crenshaw, 1991). Given an individual's multiple and intersecting identity positions, the individual can belong to multiple privileged social groups at the same time. Viewing privilege such as white privilege intersectionally, however, does not mean that minoritized whites such as white women, LGBTQ whites, and whites from lower social economic backgrounds benefit less from race privilege. Leonardo (2009) contends that "it is conceptually misleading to suggest that certain white subgroups benefit *less* from race than their counterparts. . . . I argue that *all whites benefit equally from race and racism, but they do not all benefit equally from other social relations*" (p. 121). Leonardo's argument is critical and one that we the authors believe is important for understanding how interlocking systems of oppressions impact social justice.

KEY CHALLENGES

How can we best discuss concepts such as *power* and *privilege*, which are nebulous, charged, and potentially triggering? The first key challenge is that, despite good intentions and careful planning, talks about power and privilege can backfire and end up accomplishing the opposite of what is intended. Talks about power and privilege in the classroom can become unpredictable, risky, and unsettling if not alienating because these discussions attempt to expose, interrupt, and/or disrupt existing hierarchies and positions of privilege. Depending on a variety of interpersonal, contextual, and sociocultural factors, talks about power and privilege can run the risk of reinforcing, if not bolstering, the existing power structures that the conversations seek to disrupt. As Andre Lorde famously puts it, "The master's tools will never dismantle the master's house" (2007, p. 11). This challenge reminds instructors to critically examine our instructional tools, to honestly ask what is accomplished in how concepts of power and privilege are engaged in the classroom, and to willingly reflect on who benefits from such talks. Moreover, it is important to create community agreements at the beginning of the semester (see Appendix A). Co-constructing community agreements as a class is an important tool for community building; students should have a stake in what these agreements look like. Typically, students will brainstorm rules such as:

- Make space and take space—if you usually speak more, consider letting somebody else take up space.
- Don't interrupt. Take the time to formulate a thoughtful reflection and then respond.
- Listen actively with an open mind.

- Don't generalize your experiences to an entire group.
- Be open to critique. Likewise, don't be afraid to offer critique or challenge one's opinions (including the instructor's).
- Remember that we don't have to agree. Rather, work toward understandings.

These are a few examples of ground rules that may be useful in overcoming the unpredictability of the topics that become fodder for discussions in intercultural communication. This list can be expanded and edited. Know that it's important to have student buy-in and return to these ground rules when the community principles have been violated in the discussion.

Even though ground rules like these are student-driven, we ought to stand vigilant against the particular ways in which certain rules of engagement could—despite good intentions—function to silence people of color while encouraging what DiAngelo (2018) calls "white fragility" to grow. DiAngelo conceptualizes white fragility as "the *sociology of dominance*: an outcome of white people's socialization into white supremacy and a means to protect, maintain, and reproduce white supremacy" (2018, p. 113, emphasis in original). For instance, DiAngelo (2018) argues that a common guideline for building trust such as "Don't make assumptions" is functionally meaningless and could coddle white fragility when this guideline cannot be enforced or achieved because the "nature of an assumption is that you don't know you are making it" (p. 126). Considering the rules of engagement and white fragility could mean engaging the class in re-examining the ground rules before finalizing them. Further, when the ground rules fall short of facilitating the intended space for critical conversations in the classroom, revisit the ground rules with the class as needed to make necessary adjustments and adaptations.

Furthermore, Kendi (2019) questions and challenges a common assumption that "racist minds must be changed before racist policy, ignoring history that says otherwise" (p. 208). Instead, Kendi states that "critiquing racism is not activism. Changing minds is not activism. An activist produces power and policy change, not mental change" (2019, p. 209). In other words, Kendi would encourage educators who strive to be or become anti-racist activists to prioritize and lead with anti-racist course policies and practices. In the case of class ground rules, how could those rules acknowledge racial trauma and disrupt existing power relations in the classroom? Could students of color speak first, for instance? Love (2019) reminds us that anti-racist teaching works "in solidarity with communities of color while drawing on the imagination, creativity, refusal, (re)membering, visionary thinking, healing, rebellious spirit, boldness, determination, subversiveness of abolitionists to eradicate injustice in and outside of schools" (p. 2). Coming up with and enacting ground rules and course policies that have not been tried before, indeed, would require imagination, boldness, and subversive rebellion.

Institutional contexts present a second key challenge in teaching about power and privilege. For example, faculty members at institutions that prioritize profits and revenues over students' educational experiences and a public universities' charge to promote the public good can feel unsupported, if not attacked or punished, in efforts to teach students about how power and privilege function. When administrators push a color-blind, marketplace-of-ideas approach to education, instructors' values can be compromised. We recommend learning more about your rights via your union, faculty senate, or wider cases on academic freedom. Making choices about how to push boundaries becomes important in discussions about social justice work.

Third, positionality of an instructor and their willingness to be vulnerable, to be called out, and to be challenged on one's very positions of power and privilege present another set of challenge. Yea-Wen recalls an experience when co-teaching intercultural communication with a graduate teaching assistant and an advisee at the time who self-identified as a gay white male; He and Yea-Wen shared differential experiences talking about race and racism with students at a historically white institution. As a white male, the graduate instructor tended to receive comments like "You know!" from white students in discussing race and racism. Comments like "You know!" signal a shared understanding as well as a nudge to end such a conversation as quickly as possible. As a racialized Asian female, Yea-Wen had faced numerous moments of silence when discussing race and racism. The silence could signal resistance, discomfort, annoyance, and more. This example illustrates how the instructor's positionality matters in teaching and learning about power and privilege. Communicating about instructor positionalities can be an important part of discussion. For example, explaining, "As a white female in the U.S., I have experienced privilege in these ways" or noting, "As an Asian woman in the U.S., I have experienced discrimination." Moreover, modeling behavior that calls out examples of privilege and power can be important for students' learning.

Similar to the third set of challenges, students are differentially impacted by power and privilege. For some students, it is more visible and they see/understand it. For students of more privileged backgrounds, they struggle. Students belonging to privileged groups can confuse earned and unearned privilege, deny the existence of privilege, or claim reverse racism. In contrast, students belonging to oppressed groups can re-experience racism and other interlocking oppressions during those conversations, experience being triggered, or feel discouraged or disappointed. For these conversations, it is best to be clear about earned and unearned advantages. Elucidating a definition of racism as a system, rather than individual acts, for example, helps to soften conversations about white fragility and acceptance of one's own privilege. Still, it is important for students to take an inventory of their privileges and disadvantages as a way to push toward understanding of our participation in these larger systems.

STORIES FROM THE FIELD

Anjana Mudambi, University of Wisconsin-Milwaukee

My first teaching position after graduate school was as a visiting assistant professor at a PWI/SLAC; I was joining two other faculty members to round out the Communication Department. Despite my training in critical intercultural communication, looking back, I was naïve about the institutional racism in academia. At college-wide faculty meetings, I could count the faculty of color on one hand. Teaching evaluations, notoriously biased against women faculty of color, were the sole basis of evaluating instruction. The provost, a white male in his sixties who believed that young women faculty normally receive higher teaching scores, would only ever highlight students' negative comments in his annual evaluations of me. My department chair, another white male, tenured professor, supported me by presenting him with literature (that I had collected) explaining the realities of women faculty of color, especially those of us teaching about race and/or gender. The provost warned him against explicitly naming racism or sexism as a factor in my evaluations in case of a lawsuit.

I worked in this context for three years.

Every semester, my two colleagues and I team-taught the intro to communication course, each allotted three to four weeks to introduce the areas that we taught within the program. At the end of each semester, we would decide on a current event to discuss together as a case study during the last week of class, each focusing on how our sub-discipline might approach it. One semester, we chose the controversy around the Washington Redskins team name. I was up first.

Being near D.C., I knew it would be personal and was wary of accusations of bias. I therefore showed videos of two different interviews—a co-owner of the team and a Native American activist—to guide students through a discussion of how the speakers' identities, positionalities, and histories contributed to their different perspectives. As I played the video of the Native American woman, I noticed some students' reactions—eye rolling, snickering, whispering amongst each other. I heard one student mutter, "She needs to get over it." When I tried to guide them through a historical discussion of how we had treated Native Americans in this country, I heard defensiveness: "We didn't do anything." Even as I tried to work through their reactions, I felt deflated. I felt failure. I felt embarrassment at my failure unfolding before my colleagues.

When my department chair's turn came a few days later, it was apparent that he was picking up where I had left off (from a rhetorical perspective). But he began with his own personal story: I grew up in Baltimore as a Redskins fan. *Instantly, the students tuned in. They weren't snickering; they were listening. After all,* he was one of them. He was worth listening to. And I just sank deeper into my seat. My department chair used his power to the extent he could to support me against the provost. And in the classroom, he used his privilege to reach the students in a way that I never could.

Dr. Mudambi's story highlights privilege and power both in her own experience and as a classroom concept. Her examples demonstrate how unearned advantages open doors for listening and silence non-white voices. Moreover, this example should cause us to reflect on our own privileges and disadvantages as they surface in the classroom as challenges and opportunities.

PEDAGOGICAL ACTIVITIES

In the following, we describe and discuss communication tools for exposing existing power relations and making invisible privilege visible.

Privilege and Disadvantage Inventory

Inviting students to honestly and thoughtfully respond to an inventory of statements regarding privilege or disadvantage can open up a learning space for self-inspection and self-reflexivity (see Appendix B). Briefing is key to an activity like this. This inventory can also be paired with think-pair-share or small group discussions if time allows.

The Beads of Privilege

Similar to the privilege and disadvantage inventory, the beads of privilege invites students to respond to statements of privilege across social identity groups (e.g., race, gender, sexuality) in the form of collecting beads of different colors (see Appendix C). Each color represents one social identity category. The bead visibly and concretely represents one form in which privilege manifests. The cumulation of beads of various colors highlights intersectionality of identity, power, and privilege. Debriefing can further individual and collective learning.

Privilege Walk/Exercise

Physically stepping forward or backward in response to a series of statements is another way of making visible how power and privilege manifest as daily experiences (see Appendix D). Compared with the inventory of privilege and disadvantage and the beads of privilege, this activity can feel more intense as everyone lines up and responds to each statement at the same time as a group. Also, this activity can pose greater challenge to students with physical disability and requires a large enough space to implement it. At the same time, the relative intensity of the activity can instigate greater awareness of how one is socially located in relation to others such as one's classmates.

Monopoly and Ms. Monopoly

Communication Teacher Article for Pedagogical Activities: "They'd Better Hope for a Lot of Free Parking": Using *Monopoly* to Teach about Classical Liberalism, Marginalization, and Restorative Justice."

***Ms. Monopoly is now an option:** Listen to the hosts of an NPR podcast, *The Indicator from Planet Money*, play Ms. Monopoly: https://www.npr.org/2020/01/27/800157576/the-indicator-plays-ms-monopoly.

VIDEOS AS TEACHING TOOLS

Let's Get to the Root of Racial Injustice—Professor Megan Ming Francis offers a personal story about racial injustice and debunks common "fixes" to the root causes of racial injustices. This video can supplement discussions about privilege in relation to racial (in)justice.

Tim Wise on Power, Race, and Privilege—Antiracist essayist and educator Tim Wise speaks at the University of San Francisco about unearned advantages for white bodies in a variety of context.

DISCUSSION QUESTIONS

1. How is privilege "invisible"?
2. To what extent is privilege something a person can "give up" or "give away"?
3. What is the difference between earned and unearned advantages?
4. In what ways are you privileged/disadvantaged? How has this/does this change over time?
5. Are we responsible for the actions of our ancestors? To what extent?
6. What can we do with our privilege?

Chapter 3

Negotiating Avowed and Ascribed Identities for Social Justice

Identity issues permeate across various levels of intercultural communication— from the micro to the macro, and from human to mediated communication. Therefore, it is clear that identity remains a central topic within intercultural communication.

(Bardhan & Orbe, 2012, p. xiii)

We return to "identity" and "culture for relocation, linked to political practice— identity that is not informed by a narrow cultural nationalism masking continued fascination with the power of the white hegemonic other. Instead identity is evoked as a stage in a process wherein one constructs radical black subjectivity.

(hooks, 1990, p. 20)

Reflection in the Intercultural Communication classroom gives us the opportunity to think about who we are (and/or who we want to become) and how we perceive others. Broadly, this concept of the ways in which we perceive ourselves and others and how others perceive us is referred to as *identity*. In our research, intercultural educators across paradigms agreed that identity and identity work should be a core component of intercultural communication curricula. However, the definition of the term varies across classrooms, perspectives, and goals. Moreover, related concepts can make it difficult to present a full understanding of the nuances of identity(ies) in the classroom. Is it identity or identities? Does adding the word "cultural" to make cultural identity change its definition? What about subjectivities? Do we have an identity or do we create one? Or do we co-create identities together? If so, what does co-creating identities entail, and why is that the case? When it comes to communicating identities for promoting social justice, what do we need to do individually and collectively to achieve that? These are all challenging, yet important questions that might arise when teaching the unit. These questions reflect ongoing conversations in the field.

BACKGROUND

The concept of *identity* boils down to how each of us comes to know, experience, or understand our sense of self vis-à-vis others around us. Ultimately, questions about identity are inherently related to questions about relationships between individuals, cultural groups, and their societies. In essence, an intercultural lens affords a useful juxtaposition of how two or more cultures approach and understand the concept of identity. Such juxtaposition creates a window to simultaneously better understand our own culture's perspective while learning about another culture's view. For instance, most Western societies conceive the self as an autonomous center of awareness, emotion, and action striving for purpose and volition in life. Further, the dominant Western view of the individualistic self makes clear distinctions between the self and the other. Informed by insights from intercultural educators and scholars as well as our own research, we present in the following space what we consider a synthesized version of intercultural insights on identity for teaching for social justice. We craft our version carefully to meet several goals: (a) digging into the breadth and depth of intercultural communication research on identity; (b) focusing on relevant concepts for social justice work; and (c) articulating pedagogical opportunities for teaching identity more fully.

THREE PRIMARY PERSPECTIVES ON IDENTITY

The theoretical framework used to understand identity has shifted over the years. It has been used to explain group membership (Hecht, Jackson, & Pitts, 2005), a person's unified sense of self (Cote & Levine, 2002), or a term that considers one's sociohistorical positioning (Mendoza, Halualani, & Drzewiecka, 2002; Moon, 1996). Each perspective on identity is useful to understand our sense of self and our relation to the world. Three major perspectives addressed in common intercultural textbooks (e.g., Martin & Nakayama, 2018) are social scientific, interpretive, and critical approaches to culture.

Ting-Toomey's (2003) theory of identity negotiation theorizes the process of identity negotiation in intercultural environments. Specifically, she argues that individuals must feel a secure sense of self-identification in order to feel comfortable in intercultural communication situations. Moreover, the more secure an individual is in their self-identification, the more likely they are to be interculturally competent and willing to negotiate their identity through intercultural interaction.

Interpretive interculturalists more often use *cultural identity* to articulate the ways that perceptions and understandings of an individual as a group member are imposed or produced by other individuals, groups, or public texts. Cultural identities might be made up of social categories such as race, nationality, ethnicity, sex, gender, sexuality, age, class, religion, or ability. Cultural identity theory (CIT), as it first arose in the field, argued that identities (plural) are negotiated through communication. Moreover, through this lens, identities are negotiated on the basis of scope, salience, and intensity. Cultural identity theory emphasizes **ascribed** and **avowed** identities—those given to us and those taken up by us (Collier & Thomas, 1988). Together, the assumptions of this theory offer a number of ways in which identities become important in interactions, especially intercultural interactions.

Critical intercultural theorists have moved toward critiquing the seemingly unified sense of self embedded in the singular word *identity*. Collier (2005) offers the term *identifications* as a way of moving beyond the singularity, yet still recognizes the sharedness of "locations and orientations" (p. 237). In cultural identifications, identities are both personal and political, ascribed and avowed, and exist within multiple contexts (Collier, 2005). Similarly, Mendoza, Halualani, and Drzewiecka (2002) argue that identity must always be looked at as dynamic, contextual, and always in relation to power. These critical approaches to identity theorize the construct less as fixed or simply shared with group members, but rather as a multifaceted, evolving process in which individuals are continually (re)constructed through communication.

These three perspectives are not neat boxes within which identity can neatly fit. Research spans these perspectives, moves beyond them, and can take up space within the borders of each perspective. Collier (2014), for example, articulates the value of critical interpretive approaches, in order to both understand and critique when conceptualizing identity within various contexts.

When teaching about identity in intercultural communication, one must first make a choice about which perspectives they will present. In our interviews with intercultural communication faculty, the majority of respondents said that they choose to survey the three approaches for two reasons: (1) Presenting multiple approaches to culture and identity allows students to choose which approach they wish to align with, subsequently drawing in multiple perspectives and positionalities in the audience; (2) Surveying earlier, social scientific work on identity creates a foundation for students to use the critical paradigm to make critiques—something they cannot do without first understanding what alternative arguments have been made.

An alternative approach is to choose a particular definition and set up theories to present to the class. An instructor might choose to do this if they are using an overarching framework for their class (e.g., human rights, social justice, study abroad), or if they align themselves with a particular approach. For example, one of our respondents suggested that it was easier to use critical approaches to identity in the classroom when she framed her class through a "human rights lens." Thus, the most applicable approach to identity would be one that considers context and power.

IDENTITY AND INTERSECTIONALITY

Intersectionality is a concept used to understand how social categories uniquely come together to produce complex experiences and varying levels of power and privilege (Crenshaw, 1991; Hegde, 1996; hooks, 2000, West, 2001). In other words, the social categories of race, ethnicity, nationality, sex, gender, sexuality, religion, social class, ability, and age cannot/should not be looked at as separate identity categories, but always in relation to each other. This way of looking at identities can reveal how varying levels of privilege emerge when a person is both privileged at multiple levels and marginalized at multiple levels. For example, white, straight, middle-class women might have more social status and levels of privilege when compared to a Black, lesbian women in poverty, but both may be considered somewhat marginalized when compared to white, straight, middle-class men. Intersectional investigations also are more contextually layered and relevant. For example, a comparative study on job growth between people in poverty and people in the middle class might have different results if sex, race, and nationality, along with regional histories around racism, sexism, and immigration policies are included in the study. Thus, intersectionality enables a richer view of identities and subjectivities and cultures from multiple perspectives.

KEY CHALLENGES

Teaching (about) identity can be challenging for a variety of reasons. Without space for reflection, students might focus on or feel that their identity is visible, known, and fixed. When we ask our students to tell us about their identities, they might describe one of their roles such as "I am a student"; a component of their personality, like, "I am a hard worker"; or one salient piece of their cultural identity, for instance, "I am a woman." Moreover, some students (often students occupying majority identity positions) have a difficult time grasping the notion that their identities are defined not only by the labels we apply to ourselves (avowed) but also those that are assigned to us (ascribed). For example, Brandi once had a classmate who "identified as

Black" because many of her friends identified as such, ignoring the fact that she has blonde hair, blue eyes, and white skin which can clearly be perceived by others. The instructor and fellow classmates had a very difficult time convincing her to account for her whiteness when describing her identity. Thus, the first challenge of teaching about identity is getting students to shift from *(personal) identity* to *cultural identities*, seeing their identities as complex, dynamic, multiple, fluid, and influenced by intersecting social systems and as contingent on historical contexts. We have navigated this challenge of keeping the focus on cultural identities as tied to social systems in several ways: sharing and modeling our own experiences with our salient cultural identities; inviting examples from students from minoritized groups who have to think about certain marginalized identities on a daily basis; showing and then discussing a media example; or processing this concept through a reflective activity such as cultural identity inventory.

A second challenge that presents itself in this unit is debating the relevance of social constructionism versus biological determinism (i.e., nurture vs. nature) for each identity category that makes up a person's identities. When we begin to talk about the notion that our identities are influenced by those around us and the larger discourses that we participate in, inevitably, it presents challenges to societal influence. Students might ask, "Isn't there a gay gene?" or "How can race be a social construct if it has to do with genetics?" In order to answer these questions, the communication educator must be abreast of historical contexts and be able to deconstruct the either/or binary of social constructionism as pitted against biological determinism. It is our job to talk through the arbitrary nature of language, the historical context that informs our perceptions, and evidence that demonstrates the power of our communication. Also, rather than getting stuck on the debate between either nature (biologically determined) or nurture (social constructionism), we navigate this challenge by stressing a both-and view and engaging our student in processing and thinking through what happens when different identities are marked on our bodies heavily or lightly and how communication about identities becomes an embodied experience.

In order to navigate these challenges, we proposed a reflective practice called *SWAP*ping the classroom (Chen & Lawless, 2018). Through this model instructors, facilitators, and students become co-learners committed to facilitating communication interactions that (a) *S*hift the center and the margins; (b) *W*ill oneself to listen; (c) *A*rticulate intersectional reflexivity and inquiry; and (d) *P*romote affirming communication. As the lead co-learner, the instructor takes the first step(s) in preparing the entire class to engage in collaboratively SWAPping the classroom. Given the interlocking systems of power and privilege based on race, gender, class, and others, the intellectual, emotional, and physical labor required of each member of a SWAPped classroom would vary. Ultimately, the goal of SWAPping the mainstream communication classroom is to make room for those difficult conversations that we have described earlier.

REFLECTIONS ON TEACHING CULTURAL IDENTITIES IN THE CLASSROOM

Instructors often note this unit as the most difficult to teach because, in doing so, we must broach issues of power, privilege, and marginalization (topics covered in more detail later in this book). Imagine going from teaching outlining in public speaking, to navigating conversations about race relations and structural and institutionalized racism in intercultural communication. It takes practice, time, and courage. Instructors must build a repertoire of responses to various "isms" that could emerge in these conversations. Here are some frequently asked questions and some helpful responses that may help alleviate these challenges:

Q: I'm a white instructor. How can I talk about race if I don't understand what it's like to be a person of color?

First, it is important to acknowledge, name, and identify white as a race as a starting place to make visible the system of whiteness (a.k.a. white supremacy). Even though whites and people of color alike experience becoming and being *racialized*, the particularity of racialization as whites involves ignorance, obliviousness, and denial of white supremacy. Racialization is "the process by which skin color, or any other physical attribute, becomes imbued, over time, with social, cultural, psychological, socioeconomic, and/or political significances" (Teranishi & Briscoe, as cited in Dowd & Bensimon, 2015, p. 1). Thus, naming and identifying white as a race is a critical first step. Talking about the social construction of whiteness can help bring white students on board a discussion about race. Be open and honest about your experiences, how you came to understand the world, and why you believe it is important to understand others' perspectives. In particular, white instructors occupy an advantageous position to talk about racism and whiteness with white students. It's also important to consider that for many students of color, race has been a topic that has stayed off-limits in their classroom, despite race being an important part of their lived realities. As a white instructor, consider what you are willing to offer or do when you microaggress students of color. One particularly hurtful and harmful scenario is when a white instructor responds to a racist or discriminatory comment in class with silence, which makes that silence discriminatory. See Covarrubias's (2008) piece for what she calls "masked silence sequence." It is important for all instructors to make visible intersectional privileges and disadvantages and to open up discussion about the ways in which we are communicated to/about based on avowed and ascribed identities, particularly race. That said, it is important to be humble and open to critique. Howard's (2016) article may be helpful in further explaining why it's important for the white majority of teachers to be culturally and racially conscious as they enter the classroom.

Q: *I don't want to speak for any marginalized identities in the class, but I don't want to call on these students and ask them to speak for their identity group either. What do I do?*

The best thing you can do is create a community of respect by establishing ground rules at the start of your course, foster a sense of openness, and demonstrate that you are willing to listen. The ground rules should make clear what is accepted and what is not accepted (e.g., interrupting others, using racial slurs). By creating space for discussion and dialogue, and pointing out when students say things that may marginalize others in the classroom, you work to decenter whiteness in the classroom and re-center marginalized voices. This can be bolstered with thoughtful development of the syllabus that includes readings from scholars of color, international scholars, and other intersectional identities. Make sure that the identities in your classroom are reflected in the readings you assign. You might even consider starting discussion with space for those who normally don't get a chance to speak or share their experiences. For example, if you assign a reading about the intersections of race and class, you can start class by saying, "For the first ten minutes, I'd like to open up the space for individuals who came from lower/working-class backgrounds to share, if they'd like to, how this reading resonated with their experiences. Also, people of color will speak before white people." Consider what you are willing to do should students from marginalized backgrounds become injured in your classroom.

Q: *My student, though well-intentioned, made a racist/sexist/homophobic comment. How do I navigate this without shutting them down?*

Regardless of whether or not a student was well intentioned, communication has material consequences for those who are invoked by its meaning. These instances need to be acknowledged and corrected by the instructor due to the power they carry in the classroom in relation to other students. It's ok to say, "While I understand you were coming from a good place when you made that statement, it can be perceived as homophobic/racist/sexist/ and so forth because _____." You might even ask the class how they perceived the communication and use the discussion as a learning opportunity or teachable moment. Creating opportunities like this depends on clear ground rules that are made in the beginning of the semester. Making it clear that you may make clarifications for the purpose of learning, and growing as a community makes it easier for people to be vulnerable and have some humility in these moments. We have also found it useful to introduce Johnson's (2006) *paths of most and least resistance* in communication about privilege, power, and difference. These concepts encourage students to call out microaggressions or other acts of discrimination, regardless of how small, as a way to improve communication overall.

Q: Students are having a hard time understanding that race is a social construct because it's visible. How can I teach this more clearly?

The social construction of race is one of the hardest concepts for (white) students (or anybody) to grasp because of the ways we have been taught to define race as visible—phenotype, skin color, hair texture, and so on. This discussion requires a deep dive into history to discuss the origin of "race" and how various races have been defined and altered over time. Moreover, a discussion of the census might highlight how arbitrary racial delineation is, who gets to create such categories, and how/why they are enforced. For instance, the 2010 Census treated Hispanic as an ethnicity and required all self-identified Hispanics to select a racial category (e.g., white, Black, Asian).

It is also extremely important to note that just because race has been socially constructed over time does not mean that there isn't deep cultural importance to racial labels and group membership. This is where a deeper conversation about avowal and ascription becomes important. We can ask, "Across racial groups, what are some social implications and/or consequences of being ascribed a certain race such as white, Black, or Native American? Why does an avowed identity of "Black" carry such weight if the ascribed identity of "Black" is socially constructed?" Questions, such as this one, highlight the importance of group membership, avowed identity, and histories for cultural groups. Also, the ongoing Black Lives Matter Movement serves as an invaluable example to talk about the power and social construction of race in the U.S. society.

STORIES FROM THE FIELD

Gust Yep, San Francisco State University

In the early 1990s when I was an assistant professor doing a presentation in Chinatown about culture, sexual practices, and HIV/AIDS, I still remember an incident. There was a very attentive man in the audience who came up after the presentation to ask me a question that haunted me. I use the word haunting very specifically here. He said, "You described Asian Americans in these specific ways." (I was essentially using Hofstede and Hall, referring to collectivism, high context, and the different dimensions of cultural variability.) He said, "Do you identify as Asian American?" I said "Sort of," and then he said, "Would you describe yourself that way? Like you described it in your research?" I answered his question in the context of the study, saying, "Well this is about the specific survey that I did with this specific population, this is my sample size, this is what I found and so on." I knew that he was not completely satisfied with my answer. I said "Am I answering your question?" and he politely said yes, thanked me, and left. I never actually had a chance to thank him, but the question haunted me—the question "Would I describe myself the way that intercultural communication research was describing Asians or Asian Americans?" If I were to be honest I would say no. I would not say that "I'm always high context, I'm always collectivistic, I am always high power distance, and so forth." No. It depends on context, it depends on the type of relationship, it depends on other dynamics, it depends on politics, right? So, when I started thinking about what I said, well, a lot of the research that was happening at that time was creating kind of intercultural stereotypes.

Professor Yep's story from the field demonstrates a deeply reflective moment in which he was confronted with an opportunity to rethink his avowed identity within broader contexts outside of the traditional research conducted in intercultural communication. It also highlights the challenge pointed out earlier—that all identities are fluid, dynamic, and complex. The story highlights the problem with teaching identities as fixed and essentialized. Though he is a professor, and was at the time, such scenarios are common amongst students who want a "recipe" for how to understand cultures and identities. Thus, self-reflexivity is key in deconstructing grand narratives about singular identities that neatly fit into a set of boxes.

Alberto González, Bowling Green University

In my classes, I attempt to disrupt the notion that our identities are stable and individually determined. Inspired by Dolores V. Tanno (2016) who describes how her heritage gets renamed over time, I describe my own "names over time." I move through a progression of labels and what they emphasize beginning with Spanish American (language), then Mexican (migrant stream origin), Mexican American (born in the United States), Chicano/La Raza (political activism), Hispanic (government label), Mestizo (indigenous roots), Latina/o (binary gender inclusion), Latin@ (combination of a/o to represent gender inclusion plus postmodern awareness), and now Latinx (nonbinary sexual orientation). As a Midwesterner, I relate differently to these labels than if I was from South Texas or California. It's important for you to know that we are not a monolith and that the positionality of our identity and our political emphases have varied over time.

One time, a Mexican American (as she identifies) student from South Texas enrolled in our graduate program. She began to notice that many of the Latinx people she encountered would have ball caps or t-shirts that proclaimed something about their heritage. Maybe they identified as Mexican American or Puerto Rican or Dominican. She asked me, "Why do y'all do that?" I said it was because we were a minority here in Northwest Ohio and we want people to know that we are here and that we belong as much as anyone else. She replied, "Where I'm from, we are the majority. I don't have to go to my homeland, I'm always in it. Now I'm away from it." Soon after, she wore a cap that said, "La Raza."

So, making assumptions about where someone is from or how they relate to their heritage can spell disaster. I share this story with my students. I was still relatively new at my university, but I became department chair. There was an associate dean in my college office named Adrian Tío. My wife and I decided to invite him and his wife for dinner. We made a great homemade dinner of guacamole and salsa, three cheese enchiladas con pollo, Mexican-style rice, frijoles, and my favorite Mexican beer, Tecate.

Dr. Tío was Puerto Rican. I was so embarrassed! He was very gracious. At one point he said, "Oh, you Mexicans, you put cilantro in everything." It was hilarious.

In class, I have a slide that gives a quote from my daughter Monica, the philosopher barista. She says, "If, in the course of the history of societies, our only contribution is the breakfast taco, I'm okay with that." Of course, Monica is also the one who, as a kid, got tired of eating tacos, burritos, tamales, and tostadas, all of which you can eat with your hands. "Please mom and dad," she asked, "can we eat something that uses a fork?"

Assumptions about identity are a starting point for inquiry. Assumptions generate questions: Where does this assumption come from? What does it say about how I think and who I am? What does this assumption include? What does it leave out or ignore? Who benefits from this assumption? Who is harmed by this assumption? How can I learn about an identity beyond this assumption? If the assumption is harmful, how do I work against it in my talk and writing?

As we learn, we change, and we adopt—perhaps unknowingly—a new "name over time."

Dr. González's story demonstrates two important aspects of identity: (a) the complex and dynamic nature of identities, and (b) how assumptions can lead to identity incongruence between avowed and ascribed identities. By noting that the name used to describe a group of people is constantly evolving, Dr. González also draws attention to the un/shared nature of such labels.

Avowed identities may differ amongst people of a group, leading to incorrect assumptions and intercultural communication failures. Moreover, these assumptions can lead to incorrect ascriptions, resulting in microaggressions, or lowered self-esteem for those whose identities were mis-ascribed and/or misunderstood. These are important examples for students to consider when examining their own communication practices.

PEDAGOGICAL ACTIVITIES

In addition to the reflective practices suggested before, we offer several activities that can guide discussion about identities and promote a better understanding of the fluid, complex, and dynamic nature of intersecting identities.

Cultural Identity Pyramid

Cultural Identity Pyramids are a common exercise used within classrooms and intercultural training settings (see Appendix E). This worksheet helps students to participate in a process of reflexivity and consciously consider their avowed and ascribed identities. Moreover, this activity is useful in demonstrating the relevance of salience. Identity Pyramids help students to understand that an identity is not innate, but is both created through individual understandings of self and others' perceptions of us.

Six-Word Memoirs

This published activity (see Simmons & Chen, 2014) asks students to identify one or two cultural identities and use six words to describe themselves, later reflecting on why they made these specific choices. The activity is useful in debriefing salience, self-perception, and the social construction of identities.

Exploring Diversity through Dialogue: Avowed and Ascribed Identities

In this published exercise (see Antony, 2016) students are asked to recall harmful/hurtful scenarios in which one of their cultural identities (e.g., race, class, gender) was questioned, stereotyped, or degraded. Students then discuss with a peer what happened, what was upsetting, and how the situation made them feel. Finally, students create posters that reject this hurtful communication and explain to the class how these posters speak to harmful ascribed communication. See Appendix F for using two pie charts to process avowals and ascriptions.

Autobiography of a Racialized Body

This assignment, adapted from McKinney (2008; embedded in Appendix G) encourages students to reflect on their own racial and/or ethnic heritage, including the in/visibility of such identity categories, and the ways in which intersectionality informs these identifications. The assignment shifts students thinking away from opinions about current racial issues to an introspective look at their own personal experiences with race. Students reflect on their earliest and/or most salient experiences with race and how it informs their worldviews.

Intercultural Interaction Paper

This assignment (embedded in Appendix H) is designed to aid students in reflecting on their own intercultural interactions with individuals who are not U.S.-born citizens. Students interview or participate in a conversation with someone who is studying abroad, an immigrant to the United States, a visitor/tourist, or a dual citizen. If teaching the course outside of the United States, these guidelines can be adjusted accordingly. In the conversation, students learn more about cultural differences, hidden histories, stereotypes, and other experiences related to course concepts. Findings are presented in a formal writing assignment.

Intercultural Reading Circles

Between the World and Me by Ta-Nehisi Coates is a moving letter written from a Black father to his son about what it is like to grow up as a Black man in the United States. The author uses statistics and personal experiences to paint a picture about how Black bodies are perceived, stereotyped, and repeatedly violated in a society that insists it is post-racial. Student discussion can draw from Coates's examples to articulate an understanding of ascribed identities, context, and power in identity construction, and intersectionality.

The Color of Water: A Black Man's Tribute to His White Mother by James McBride uses prose to better understand the intersectional identity of bi-raciality. In the memoir, McBride's mother, a white Jewish woman who married a Black man in the 1940s struggles to explain race to her children, ultimately describing it as "the color of water"—ambiguous and fluid. McBride's struggle with identity is ripe for discussion about race, salience, avowed versus ascribed identities, and intersectionality.

Examples of other books can be found in the sample syllabus (Appendix H). Intercultural reading circles can be expanded into a final assignment in which students critically analyze the messages of popular press books related to identity and intercultural communication and apply course concepts.

VIDEOS AS TEACHING TOOLS

Actions are illegal, never people: Jose Antonio Vargas, an award-winning journalist, an activist, and the founder of "Define American," stories his journey as an undocumented immigrant born in the Philippines and immigrated to the United States with his grandfather at the age of twelve. Antonio Vargas argues that immigration is one of the most controversial yet least understood issues in the U.S. society. His talk is organized around common questions that he has received around immigration. This talk is great for unpacking the intersection of politics, immigration, race, sexuality, and more.

The year I was homeless: Becky Blanton shares her journey of becoming one of the working homeless in the United States at one point of her life. Her story depicts intimate reflections on the harsh conditions of homelessness such as stigma, criminalization, and hopelessness. Blanton's talk is rich for discussing identity and subjectivity as relating to how social conditions enable and/or constrain individual identity negotiations.

What it's like to be a Muslim in America: Through sharing her lived experiences as a researcher and a practicing Muslim, Dalia Mogahed unpacks problematic perceptions of and assumptions about Muslim people and Islam as a religion (e.g., Islamophobia) in the United States and around the world. She underscores a major obstacle that most U.S. Americans don't know a Muslim personally. She ultimately encourages choosing courage and compassion over fear, panic, and prejudice.

DISCUSSION QUESTIONS

1. In your experience, to what extent is "cultural identity" biologically determined (nature) and/or socially constructed (nurture)?
2. Why is it important to make the communicative shift from identity to *identities*?
3. Why must we acknowledge and become aware of *both* avowed and ascribed identities?
4. How are negotiations of avowals and ascriptions contingent on contexts?
5. How can power relations affect one's ability to negotiate his/her/their identity avowals and ascriptions?
6. Why is it necessary to consider avowals and ascriptions in communicating for social justice?
7. In your opinion, what would it take for all of us to truly respect and celebrate each other's intersecting identities? Should constraining or subjugating ascriptions be banned, why or why not?

Chapter 4

Building Alliances

So, what are we doing and what really matters?
　Who is actually listening, who benefits from our chatter?
This doesn't feel good, this critical interrogation.
I'm not optimistic now; there's just domination.
What about this framework, critical/interpretive praxis?
And dancing with difference—where does that take us?
Toward community engagement that is inclusive and just.
Toward power with, not power over; equity not conquest.
Cultures are contradictions and itineraries in motion,
Interculturalities and intersectionalities, position in relation.
Know how the context constraints, yet know that we can move,
Our actions can change material conditions; we can improve.
Ideologies can be uncovered, looking out and in,
Alliances can mobilize and movements can begin.
This will feed our need for change and engage our spirits again.

(Collier, 2014, p. 241)

Some readers may be teaching intercultural communication in conjunction with interpersonal communication. It makes sense to examine *relationships* in the context of culture and communication. Importantly, an intercultural communication context can help us to ask, "What can relationships look like within a social justice framework?" We explore the theoretical background of intercultural alliances and key concepts that bolster the study of these alliances. We also explore microaggressions and how to engage in consciousness of our everyday taken-for-granted communication. While we find the concept of intercultural alliance appropriate for thinking about relating in the classroom context for social justice, at the same time, we must acknowledge this view that allies cannot be self-claimed but need to be earned and/or bestowed. In other words, self-claiming to be an ally is easier said than done and can do more harm than good if one has not done the necessary work in all forms. Performative or "optical allyship" is surface-level allyship that can reinforce "tokenism, white saviorism, [and] white centering" (Saad, 2020, p. 157). Allyship deserves no reward. Rather, allyship must be genuine and intentional.

BACKGROUND

As students begin/continue to explore their varying levels of privilege, it is important to place this reflexivity into relational contexts. While "ally" seems to be a buzz word for millennials and Generation Z, the concept of *intercultural alliances* is clearly laid out and well developed by communication scholars (e.g., Allen, 2012; Allen, Broome, Jones, Chen, & Collier, 2003; Carrillo Rowe, 2003; Collier 2003; Collier & Ringera, 2016; DeTurk, 2006, 2011, 2015; Lawless, 2016; Quijada, 2008) and accompanied by a set of skills that help to develop such reflexive relationships.

Intercultural alliances are different from friendships (see table 4.1). While friendships can exist on surface levels and generate on the basis of shared interests and time spent together, alliances must move to a deeper, more nuanced, and intentional level. Intercultural alliances are "those in a relationship working to achieve a goal, who have an association to further the common interests of group members . . . contingent upon each of their complex descriptions of their situated experiences and observations" (Collier, 2003, p. 7). Also important to intercultural alliances are a "shared political itinerary" (Collier & Ringera, 2016, p. 157), examination of positions of power (Carrillo Rowe, 2010), the challenging of social injustice (DeTurk, 2011), common goals and honored differences (DeTurk, 2015), and "the emergent authenticity evident in relationships that are mutually desired, built, and maintained (Lawless, 2016, p. 346). With this in mind, Collier (2003) builds

Table 4.1. Characteristics of Alliances versus Friendships

Alliances	Friendships
• Mutually beneficial • Working to achieve a goal • Situated within social/cultural contexts • Emergent authenticity • Shared political itinerary • Requires examination of power and privilege • Challenges social injustice	• No clear criteria for friendship • Based around shared interests, commonalities, and/or time together • May rely on personal chemistry or sense of belonging • Political itineraries or goals may be divergent

a strong foundation for students understanding how to form intercultural alliances.

Three Prongs of Intercultural Alliances

Mary Jane Collier's (2003) work on intercultural alliances helped to articulate how alliances are built and maintained. She offers three tenets of an intercultural alliance: (1) shared recognition of power and privilege, (2) shared recognition of histories, and (3) an orientation of affirmation.

Shared recognition of power and privilege. The literature on intercultural alliances is unanimous in declaring that participants, especially individuals in positions of power or with some level of privilege, need to be reflexive about these contexts and hierarchies. Status-based hierarchies and privilege informs relationships. Moreover, people do not have power; rather, it emerges in relationships. If building an alliance is a shared goal, then participants must work to understand how their varying levels of privilege and power inflect on each other. Files-Thompson and McConatha (2020) add that "an ally must be informed of the power of visibility. . . . Allies must educate themselves on how their own visibility in families, communities, educational systems, the state, and the media all contribute to positions of power in their own lives and how to best use this power to call for a more inclusive and representative narrative" (p. 251). For instance, in our working relationship, it is important for Brandi to recognize her privilege as a native-English-speaking, white U.S. citizen. These privileges inflect upon her relationship with Yea-Wen, a Taiwanese citizen and a U.S. permanent resident, for whom English is not her first language. Understanding such differences is important for how we write together, talk about our experiences, and advocate for our work together. More about understanding power and privilege can be read in chapter 2.

Shared recognition of histories. In conjunction with understanding individual positionalities within an intercultural alliance, it is important to have a shared understanding of how history/histories inform individual lived realities, and ultimately the relationship. By *history*, we are not referring to personal life stories (which students so often cling to). Rather, Collier (2003) asks us to consider how history/histories of marginalized groups or historical traumas impact the present and create a communication context in which we must analyze relationships. This is to say that having a study-abroad experience in the past is not akin to having the weight of Japanese internment permeating through your ancestry. Understanding one's role in reshaping the present and working toward social justice requires a more meaningful acknowledgment of past atrocities and the material consequences of historical trauma. The realities of slavery, genocide, redlining, women's suffrage, the demeaning medicalization of LGBTQ identities, and so on are all examples of histories that impact the everyday communication and lived realities of people we may be building intercultural alliances with. Recognizing, acknowledging, and being accountable for the impact of histories on our relationships improve the quality of an alliance.

Orientation of affirmation. A successful alliance is predicated on affirming one's avowed identities and meeting them where they are. This requires deep listening, empathy, and a genuine desire to be open to understanding new perspectives. As discussed in chapter 2, a person's avowed identities often differ from the ascribed identities they are given, resulting in identity incongruence (and ultimately, low self-esteem). When we affirm people's avowed identities, we communicate trust and honor the identities he/she/ze/they claim as their own. Having an orientation of affirmation means that participants in an alliance must apologize for or stand up against those who perpetrate microaggressions, even when they weren't "intentional."

The reality is that upholding and practicing the three tenets do not and cannot guarantee intercultural allyship. Alcoff (1991) cautions us against serious challenges and concerns when speaking for others even as an ally. Specifically, Alcoff reminds us to consider and analyze "the probable or actual effects of the words on the discursive and material context. One cannot simply look at the location of the speaker or her credentials to speak, nor can one look merely at the propositional content of the speech; one must also look at where the speech goes and what it does there" (p. 26). That is, speaking as an ally is limited, can become problematic, and is not enough without responsibility and accountability. Recognizing the limitation of an ally, Clemens (2017) offers the notion of "an accomplice" in activism as someone "will focus more on dismantling the structures that oppress . . . and such work will be directed by the stakeholders in the marginalized group" (para. 5). Whether the preferred term is an ally, an accomplice, or a co-conspirator, their words might not speak as loud as their concrete actions.

CONFRONTING MICROAGGRESSIONS: SOME WAYS TO BECOME AN ALLY

One area we might teach students to build alliances is when combatting microaggressions. Microaggressions are subtle, cumulative insults targeted at (often racial) minorities (Pierce, 1974; Solorzano, Ceja, & Yosso, 2000). Though used initially to describe acts of subtle racism, "microaggression" has been extended to understand everyday discrimination based on sex, gender, and sexual orientation. For example, Solorzano (1998) found that Chican@ scholars' career paths were affected by racial and gendered microaggressions.

Microaggressions have also been described for immigrant women (Lawless & Chen, 2015). Teaching a unit on microaggressions fits well in conjunction with alliances because case studies about microaggressions present opportunities for students to understand how they can be a better ally by challenging microaggressions. It is an opportunity for students to recognize power and privilege, be cognizant of histories that inform communication, and communicate from an orientation of affirmation.

An easy tool to help students challenge microaggressions is the CHANGE tool. CHANGE is an acronym that allows students to recall productive steps to avoiding and combatting microaggressive behaviors.

C = **Communicate** with others about microaggressions
H = **Hear** others when they say they have been microaggressed
A = **Acknowledge** when you perpetuate microaggressions and experience them
N = **Negotiate** differences in understanding microaggressions
G = **Grow** awareness of the social/cultural impact of microaggressions in society
E = **Engage** in difficult conversations that will help to end microaggressive behaviors

Using the CHANGE tool encourages students to be more reflexive about their own actions, while taking the path of most resistance (Johnson, 2006) by challenging harmful communication. This is just one example of how discussions of alliance building can be paired with case studies (see Appendix I) regarding communication. For more communication research on microaggressions, see a special issue edited by Harris and Moffitt (2019) published by the *Southern Communication Journal* that features essays addressing and highlighting how communication can perpetuate, process, and/or respond to race-based microaggressions.

KEY CHALLENGES

At first glance, teaching about intercultural alliances may seem less complicated than some of the other topics we cover in this book. However, it is this seeming ease that makes it a challenge in the classroom. It is easy to conflate the term "alliance" with "friendship," without doing the work to be reflexive about power and privilege or learning about traumatizing histories that inform a person's day-to-day experiences. For that reason, we think it is important and strongly recommend covering this topic *after* units on identity, power, and privilege in order to more concretely apply the concepts and make these differentiations. This also creates a great opportunity for assessing students' understandings of previous course content.

Another challenge to teaching about intercultural alliances is getting students to think about failure and their own shortcomings when it comes to being an ally. Building strong alliances moves beyond claiming the title "ally" and implicates students in the larger work of social justice. Getting students to not just think about how they have been successfully building alliances but also where they can improve or how they have fallen short in the past is a difficult but challenging task. For example, the positionality of an ally can be precarious since allies could potentially flee accountability, responsibility, and more when the going gets tough. Thus, to what extent might alliance be liminal? What difference, if any, might it make if we shift our language from "ally" to "co-conspirator" or "accomplice"? We recommend the "Alliance Building Reflection Paper" in the pedagogical activities to help broach this subject.

Finally, we have found the concept of "histories" to be a challenging concept for students who are new to the study of intercultural alliances. Often, we find students claiming to be analyzing history, while recounting individual narratives of themselves or people they are forming relationships with (e.g., describing the childhood of a friend and how it differed from their own). Clarifying this principle by talking about systemic histories or social histories and providing adequate examples helps to re-shift this focus for students who find the concept confusing.

STORIES FROM THE FIELD

Mary Jane Collier, Colorado State University

Engaging in research and praxis with intercultural alliances has been a major source of challenge, learning, and connection. Given the pervasive contested political, cultural, economic, and social landscape, applications of critical pedagogy to intercultural conflict, community engagement, and social justice are desperately needed today. My story focuses on a two-day, overnight retreat for a course in intercultural conflict and community building, which is an ideal space to engage students in intercultural alliances.

There are several key concepts that guide my intercultural alliance activity design. There are different levels of intercultural alliances, including dyadic, intragroup, or intergroup relationships. These associations of allies are able to act in service of social justice, political/social change, or conflict transformation. Note that allies are not necessarily friends, but individuals and groups collaborating with a political itinerary such as anti-racism or conflict transformation.

One retreat activity the first day enabled dyads to explore their experiences of intercultural conflict with an ally. After individually filling out a worksheet about an intercultural conflict and their varied identities (both avowed and ascribed), pairs did a "walk-about dialogue." They shared perspectives about each other's conflict and discussed how their learnings might enable new approaches to the conflict.

A simulation, a town hall meeting over a neighborhood conflict, focused on forming intragroup and intergroup alliances. The cultural groups included undocumented residents, apartment managers, college students, police, and city council representatives. Participants within each group developed alliances through presenting concerns, visions, and recommended actions. Later, groups could send a representative to another group to propose an intergroup alliance, followed by an opportunity for those two groups to meet. Another simulation, a public forum on forest land management, also involved cultural groups presenting their interests and goals to the large group, and then proposing areas of common interest and action plans that would feature intergroup alliances. Some groups joined alliances, others did not.

Other key concepts are that there are many stories, many voices, and cultural struggles; alignments across individuals, subgroups, groups, and communities are plural, contested, intersecting, and contextually negotiated. This makes setting up simulations more complex, but also increases the relevance and validity of the experiences.

Incorporating attention to the role of macro, meso, and micro contextual features on intercultural alliances is essential. In debriefing discussions, as well as a retreat reflection paper, students were asked to talk about contextual factors. Students were also asked to bring in critical reflexivity, to question the influence of their own cultural locations and privilege as well as understanding that relating as intercultural allies is a dance between partners who must negotiate different contexts and settings and move with each other in multiple ways, sometimes inviting others in, other times stepping back.

Students come to see that intercultural alliances are not a magic tool to achieve social change. The structures and systemic practices that produce and sustain conflict and struggle for resources have long histories. Alliances are not feasible for all groups since all parties have to weigh the benefits and consequences of the relationships.

Finally, the retreat place, time, and space matter. When students and facilitators gather for two days in a natural setting, and retreat activities are designed to build trust to enable openness, critique, moving into conflict, and connection through alliances, richer reflections and deeper conversations are enabled. These increase students' appreciation of the types, challenges, and potential value of intercultural alliances to address some of the myriad conflicts existing today.

Dr. Collier's story takes teaching outside of the classroom and envisions a different context for learning. The retreat experience that she describes remarkably demonstrates the use of time, space, and silence as tools for building *deep* relationships and embracing contemplative practices. Within this retreat setting, Dr. Collier offers several tools for applying the concepts related to intercultural alliances.

PEDAGOGICAL ACTIVITIES

In addition to the reflective practices suggested before, we offer several activities that can guide discussion about intercultural alliances.

Friendship versus Alliance Handout

It is common for students to conflate friendships and alliances. This handout (Appendix J) helps students to see them as separate but overlapping concepts. It is useful to complete the first part of the workshop *before* debriefing the differences as a class. Use this activity to introduce the key components of an alliance before moving to the second component, allowing students to connect the concepts to their own relationships.

Alliance Building Reflection Paper

This course assignment (Appendix K) asks students to reflect on intercultural alliances, their successes, and their failures. After introducing the core concepts of intercultural alliances, this paper assignment can be used to assess and deepen the understanding of how students communicate in personal relationships and how they can improve those relationships.

Alliance Dialogues

This activity (Appendix L) is best if facilitated after reading the article "Ally, Friend, or Mentor? Creating and Maintaining Effective Cross-Class Alliances" (Lawless, 2016). To help students think outside of international or interracial relationships as alliances, these dialogues highlight class differences. Ask students to identify how the dialogue between potential intercultural allies is problematic. Ask them to improve the dialogues through role-play.

VIDEOS AS TEACHING TOOLS

The Everyday Ally: Nina G. describes herself as "America's only stuttering female stand-up comedian." Her talk explores microaggressions against the disabled and describes how to be an ally for the disabled.

Allyship is the Key to Social Justice: Whitney Parnell, CEO of Service Never Sleeps, provides examples of allyship and why it must be linked to social justice. She begins her talk with her musical single, "The Talk," a song about being Black in America in the context of police shootings of unarmed African Americans. She defines allyship as "an active way of life."

A Toolkit for Becoming a Trans Ally: Dr. Eli Green, the founder of the Transgender Training Institute explores the connection between fear and hate. He shares his personal story about what it means to be transgender and offers tools for being an ally to transgender people.

Building True Allies: Nikki Silvestri, the executive director of Green for All, explains how principles of allyship relate to social organizing, particularly food insecurity. She describes the tenets of being a good ally as (1) reflecting people back to themselves, (2) the art of *being with*, (3) intention versus impact, and (4) responsibility without shame.

DISCUSSION QUESTIONS

1. How are intercultural alliances different from friendships? What are the defining features of an intercultural alliance?
2. Why is it important to understand one's own positions of power and privilege as part of an intercultural alliance?
3. What might intercultural alliances look like when we consider intersectionality?
4. Why must intercultural alliances be mutually beneficial, by definition?
5. Give an example of a time when you failed to create an intercultural alliance. What went wrong? How could the alliance be successfully strengthened?

Chapter 5

Community Engagement for Social Justice

How do we as critical educators address students as moral agents in a context where there is an (inter)cultural imperative to act responsively and responsibly? I think it is first important that we fully experience this communal and collective imperative to act ourselves.

(Cooks, 2017, p. 42)

[Community Action Pedagogy] constitutes an activist communication education that addresses directly social justice problems, seeking to develop an educated activist class, by inspiring students beyond matriculation to develop their roles as activists and to support activist communities and social justice initiatives.

(Frey & Palmer, 2017, p. 363)

Our greater awareness of ourselves and others is enacted on a larger social level, in which we consider policies, social movements, and larger peace processes. Community building is an essential and indispensable aspect of teaching/learning for social justice. Striving for justice for all is a communal effort that requires buy-in, dedication, and commitment from everyone. This chapter reviews and describes processes and approaches for building a community for justice that honors diverse voices and affirms humanity in a deeply divisive climate.

BACKGROUND

We include a chapter on community engagement because it is one way to think beyond cultural Others and toward shared goals for diversification and justice in the intercultural communication classroom. We focus on community engagement as bridging differences for shared social goals that promote equity and justice in and beyond the classroom. Through this lens, it becomes appropriate to think of the intercultural classroom as an activist space where students and instructors are engaged in democratic processes by which we create change. This work is done for the purposes of achieving social justice—the equitable distribution of and access to resources. These are principles of intercultural communication because one's ability to participate in democratic processes and achieve social justice is inherently tied to identities and subjectivities—those categories that normalize who we are or define us as outsiders with limited access to resources. These divisions are exacerbated through dominant narratives that encourage us to think about our own resources as meritocratic rewards that should be hoarded and celebrated. The intercultural communication classroom can be instrumental in interrogating such narratives and building new communities across differences that work toward social justice.

Many of the topics we have discussed in this book happen on the interpersonal and/or intergroup level. These topics can be difficult to link to a broader, sociocultural level. Sorrells (2013) articulates frames for understanding conflict that can be applied more broadly when linking these interpersonal/intergroup topics to larger social structures and policies. Sorrells offers "micro," "meso," and "macro" frames for understanding (see table 5.1), urging students and researchers to consider intercultural factors that range from cultural orientations and communication style to geopolitical power inequities and colonial histories.

A macro-frame, while more abstract, is useful in introducing students to connections between tangible acts of communication and more systemic issues that inform that communication. Teaching students to not only understand what a macro-frame is, but how to apply it to micro- and meso-communication acts builds upon previous knowledge, promotes critical thinking, and works

Table 5.1. Frames for Analysis

Frames	Micro-Frame	Meso-Frame	Macro-Frame
	(Individual-Based)	(Group Based)	(Discourse and Representation)
	Things to analyze: Cultural orientation, communication style, language, conflict style, facework, situational factors	*Things to analyze:* Prejudice; ethnocentrism; racism, sexism, homophobia, etc.; cultural histories; cultural identities; power imbalance	*Things to analyze:* Media; economic factors; political factors; geopolitical power inequities (e.g., history of colonization, imperialism, hegemony)

Source: Adapted from Sorrells (2013).

toward social change. After students develop a strong understanding of context, structures, and identities, and other communication processes, they are better equipped to "intervene directly into unjust discourses to promote social justice" (Frey & Palmer, 2014, p. 9). It is these connections that form a foundation for community engagement for justice.

Activism in the Intercultural Classroom

Intercultural communication does need to be envisioned as one in which teachers lead protests with their students. Rather, when we talk about activism in the classroom, we refer to civic engagement that uses the tools and analytic foundation learned in the intercultural classroom to engage in broader social issues in our communities. Students should be prepared to engage in the difficult conversations that impact their daily lives and ask, "How is my well-being wrapped up in the well-being of those in this community? How do local policies and systems reinforce inequitable distribution of and access to resources in my community? How can I intervene in and/or challenge these structures?" With a foundational understanding of difference, inequity, and social justice, students can engage these larger questions.

Activism is politically charged and even taboo when applied to the college classroom. Still, we argue that activism inherently belongs in the intercultural communication classroom. Indeed, activist pedagogies can prove useful in teaching students how to apply the skills they have learned. Frey and Palmer (2014) argue this scaffolding is essential for teaching toward justice, stating,

> *Communication activism pedagogy* (CAP) teaches students how to use their communication knowledge and resources (e.g., theories, research methods, pedagogies, and other practices) to work together with community members to intervene into and reconstruct unjust discourses in more just ways. (p. 8)

Politics, then, needs to be a discussion arena we are willing to traverse. Our pedagogies must be "politically informed," providing us with a tool belt "to enable students to understand systemic structures and practices that create and maintain injustice" (Frey & Palmer, 2014, p. 2).

In our research (2019), it was commonly acknowledged that teaching from social scientific and interpretive perspectives are easier and less exhausting for the instructor and students. In other words, introducing students to categorical theories and relatable theories of intercultural transitions (e.g., U-curve, culture shock) is less challenging and political. However, many instructors felt the need to move toward more critical and activist approaches in order to encourage students to challenge the social structures that keep cultural groups and individuals marginalized. Many instructors we interviewed argued that this activist approach resulted in stronger transformation of students in the long term.

In her dialogues with social justice educators, Cooks (2017) found that "activist efforts such as (at the time) #BlackLivesMatter were seen as informational pedagogical examples, rather than as potential catalysts for getting students involved in change" citing participants' concerns for their careers if they were to condone and utilize activism in the classroom (p. 28). Despite these concerns, Cooks' participants recognized an "(inter)cultural imperative to act responsively and responsibly," leading Cooks to argue that intercultural communication curriculum must take an ethical, and therefore, activist stance (p. 29). Such an approach offers a call to action and a chance for students and instructors to address this call both as individuals and as a collective.

Community-Engaged Learning

Working with communities, while challenging, can bolster the experience of intercultural communication. Community-engaged learning[1] can help to build empathy, uncover cultural biases, and form relationships that extend beyond the classroom (Blithe, 2016). Moreover, community-engaged learning can be used to nurture understandings of difference (Boyle-Baise, 2002). For example, students participating in community-engaged learning in the Tenderloin (low-income district in San Francisco with a large homeless population) had a stronger understanding of personal privileges, had increased awareness of systemic oppression and marginalization, and exposed their own biases and stereotype projections (Lawless, 2019). Community-engaged learning can also build campus-community relationships, and aid in mission accomplishment for local community organizations. This creates an opportunity for students to participate in local activism, policy making, and community organizing, while learning about cultural Others.

Community-engaged learning creates one type of opportunity for students to connect their understanding of culture(s) and intercultural communication to broader social structures and policies. Such activities also reinforce material learned in class because "drawing students out of the classroom environment and infusing them into marginalized communities exposes students to systematic and lived conditions of injustice and oppression" (Frey & Palmer, 2014, p. 25).

In addition to the reinforcement and transformative effects of community-engaged learning, this form of community building can shift the focus away from a savior complex or one that marks charitable giving as the solution to the world's injustices. Rather, students should be able to "see social problems as products of imbalances in political and economic power that can be directly challenged through communication activism" (Frey & Palmer, 2014, pp. 25–26).

Several teacher-scholars have documented their experiences of teaching intercultural communication through a community-engaged framework (Blithe, 2016; Borden, 2007; De Leon, 2014; Endres & Gould, 2009; Kennerly, 2014). Overall, these assessments find that a community-engaged approach reduces ethnocentrism, promotes social transformation, and improves attention to issues of power and privilege. Kennerly (2014) detailed her experiences with a community-engaged learning structure for intercultural communication, requiring students to conduct intercultural field research about a cultural group that was "significantly different from their culture" (p. 335). She found that this approach was useful in building depth of knowledge, but also in responding to anti-immigrant discourse or building on other themes of the course. Blithe (2016) was able to use this approach to produce digital storytelling projects based on community members' experiences. She also found students awareness of larger hegemonic structures increased.

In our own courses, we have used community-engaged learning as one tool to build upon intercultural communication theories and processes and work toward understandings of macro issues affecting intercultural groups. Lawless (2019) documents how Street Retreats, which immerse students in a community with a large homeless population, resulted in "realization of personal privileges," "shifts in bias/stereotype projection," "shifts in levels of dis/comfort," and "shifts in awareness and consciousness" (pp. 548–551). In fall 2015, Yea-Wen partnered with Asian Community Alliance to engage students in a relatively more open-ended service-learning project due to the physical distance between Athens and Cincinnati, Ohio (approximately 160 miles). Students worked in groups responding to a prompt provided by the community partner to collect accounts, stories, and narratives from Asian and Asian American students at their university regarding their views of and experiences with communication and violence: *"How can we better communicate with members of the Asian and Asian American communities regarding issues of violence (such as sexual assault and domestic violence)? What works? What does not? What are particular needs around these issues?"* The process of developing and working on their service-learning projects afforded everyone involved opportunities to examine and reflect on issues of (in)visibility, stereotypes, and stigmas in relation to Asians and Asian Americans.

KEY CHALLENGES

Broadly, the optics of an "activist" pedagogy can be problematic as it exists within broader discourses that define education as apolitical. Educators are urged to avoid politics, not to get on a soapbox, and remain neutral. Yet, all education is political and the status quo represents dominant ways of knowing and doing (Shor, 1993). If our project is to teach about the inequitable distribution of and differential access to resources, then we must be able to describe the inequities that affect the communities and cultures we are studying. Still, we push up against these expectations that such topics can and should be avoided in the classroom. These expectations are reinforced not only by administrators, but by students as well—some more overtly than others.[2] As instructors, we ourselves might unknowingly buy into or internalize such expectations, especially early on in our career. A growing sentiment of anti-intellectualism would have us believe that we must present a marketplace of ideas, where students can choose the knowledge(s) they like best. Consider that this might be dangerous and "antithetical to the role and purpose of higher education" (Lawless, Rudick, & Golsan, 2019, p. 485). Alternatively, informed political pedagogies work to "rigorously produce, test, and disseminate knowledge and curriculum that elevates public discourses and informs decision-making and, conversely, to eliminate or recall those ideas that are harmful" (p. 487). Developing these politically informed pedagogies and introducing them in the classroom, while challenging, is necessary for battling the rampant anti-intellectualism of the current political moment and creating long-term change for individuals from marginalized backgrounds. This is our intellectual and pedagogical responsibility as instructors of intercultural communication for social justice. Ultimately, if we are not actively exposing social inequalities in our classes and unpacking cultural politics that (re)produce, if not widen, existing gaps, then we are teaching to maintain the status quo. With that said, the burden, labor, and potential risk of practicing politically informed pedagogies fall differentially on instructors of intercultural communication across race/ethnicity, sex and gender, class, sexuality, and more. Considering that intercultural communication is a political project, we recommend navigating this intricate challenge by focusing on social-justice issues that you as a teacher-scholar care about and/or you find intimately affect your students' lives.

We have offered community-engaged learning as one example of a way to connect micro and meso-understandings of culture to broader, macro-levels of understanding. Some of the most transformative learning can happen when working with/in the community. Yet, this opportunity comes with great challenges. Campus constraints including class size, time and space, and budget make it difficult to build meaningful and long-lasting community relationships. We realize that this approach puts more labor on the instructor and creates greater labor for community partners. This increased labor is often not compensated or supported by our institutions, and there are few roadmaps for how to develop strong and long-lasting relationships between academics and the community. Questions such as "How do I find a community partner to work with?" "How do I get students into the community during a class that meets for fifty minutes?" and "How can I get students excited about this work?" are difficult to answer, especially when resources are not readily available on campus. Here are some questions to help navigate such challenges:

Community Partners

- Do you have a center on campus that already has relationships with local nonprofit or community organizations?
- Do you have personal relationships with leadership in local community organizations?
- Can your students reach out to local community organizations?
- Are there resources on campus for compensating community partners?
- What are your goals for this project? How do they align with the community partner's goals?
- Can you work with multiple community partners to meet different student needs?
- Is this work mutually beneficial? If not, how can you make it so for an already overworked community partner?

Time and Space Constraints

- Is there (free) access to public transportation from campus?
- What organizations are within walking distance to campus?
- Can you include lab or service hours in the course for additional credit hours?
- Is there a project that you could swap out that would take the same number of out-of-class hours?
- Can you use class time to meet with community partners?
- Have you considered rotating between meeting with partners on campus and in the community?
- Can you experiment with an intensive class format that allows for longer class periods?

Student Perceptions

- Can students choose what times they work with this community organization?
- Will students get credit or designation on their transcript for this work?
- Have you explained the benefits of community-engaged learning as an approach?
- Have you discussed the differences between volunteering and community-engaged approaches?

STORIES FROM THE FIELD

Sara DeTurk, University of Texas at San Antonio

Community Building through Structured Dialogue: I frequently teach a senior capstone course on training and group facilitation. In this class I incorporate service learning, community engagement, and intercultural communication through structured intergroup dialogue. I begin by introducing students to structured dialogue as one of several training techniques. I define dialogue as conversation aimed at understanding rather than persuasion, and the structure comes from skilled facilitation and ground rules such as active listening, showing respect, striving for a balance of listening and speaking, and speaking only for oneself. ("Intergroup" dialogue is dialogue about and across difference.)

During class I demonstrate the process through the "fishbowl" technique, where eight to twelve volunteers sit in a circle and the rest of the class observes. I propose a topic such as immigration, and invite participants to share their views using discussion prompts like "Do you think we have an immigration crisis?" and "What experiences do you have with immigrants or immigration?" Over the course of the semester, students practice facilitating structured dialogue about other controversial topics.

The culmination of students' development as facilitators is an event we organize that is open to the public and hosted by a community organization such as San Antonio's peaceCENTER or the Dialogue Institute of the Southwest. The students work together with the organization to choose the dialogue topic, plan the event (including discussion prompts and icebreakers), and promote it to the public. Typically, we also partner with our university's Multicultural Student Center for Equity and Justice to organize an on-campus event. (This gives the students more opportunities for facilitation, and is a great extra-credit opportunity for my intercultural communication students!) For students who are unable to attend either event, I work with our Center for Civic Engagement (and my own community contacts) to identify other facilitation-related service-learning opportunities.

Themes of dialogue events with community partners have included "Bridges: Dialogues around Immigration" and "Hate Hurts: Can We Disagree without Being Disagreeable?" On campus, we have addressed topics such as racism; gendered violence; body image and popular culture; U.S.–Arab communication; U.S. identity and the American dream; and merit versus access in college admission.

After our events to date, students have written reflection papers in which they expressed satisfaction with their success in applying the skills they had learned in class in the "real world." More powerfully, they described having their eyes opened about the experiences of immigrants, having their stereotypes of priests and nuns disconfirmed, and enjoying connecting with people much older than themselves. Some said they were surprised or moved by the enthusiasm of community members to come out to engage across difference, and several expressed hopes or intentions to seek out similar experiences in the future.

These experiences, in sum, helped prepare students to be leaders in fostering respectful dialogue across difference. It also exposed them to a broader community beyond the university, encouraged them to engage with people outside their own social groups, and gave them a taste for making the world a better, more peaceful place through community engagement.

Dr. DeTurk's description of incorporating service-learning and community engagement into her course demonstrates the ways in which community-engaged learning can be transformative for both students and community members. Her project demonstrates the applied nature of this form of pedagogy and the ways in which concepts from this course can be highlighted (e.g., immigration, identity, marginalization, and ideologies) and made visible/tangible for students.

PEDAGOGICAL ACTIVITIES

Community-Based Social Media Campaigns

Hanasono's (2016) semester-long project teaches students how to use social media (e.g., Twitter and Facebook) to build anti-hate campaigns that challenge stereotypes and build social support. The activity encourages students to work with local diversity initiatives and community groups in designing and managing the campaign.

Be the Change You Wish to See

This published (Alexander & Liu, 2018) semester-long assignment is designed to improve connectedness across cultural groups. Over the course of the semester, students build a habit of thinking more deeply about communication in interracial communication and reflect on insights about personal or societal communication and brainstorm actions that address those insights. Students then provide long-term "action" goals for improving communication across communities.

Observing Your Communit(ies)

This activity (see Appendix M) asks students to observe various neighborhoods/communities within a city, take field notes, and share with the class. This activity can spark discussion about disparities; rhetorics of race, class, and poverty; and community activism.

Service-Learning Journals

This assignment (embedded in Appendix G) asks students to reflect on their service-learning experience by addressing what was accomplished with their community partner(s), what knowledge was gained about self and others, connections and applications to intercultural communication concepts from class discussion, and general insights. Reflection journals are a common tool assigned in service-learning/community-engagement courses because they ask students to consciously apply course material to experiences with/in the community.

VIDEOS AS TEACHING TOOLS

Black Activism Is Changing Your Community for the Better: Cicely-Belle Blain explains how intersectional communities (such as Black Lives Matter) can work toward liberation on a societal scale. This video is useful to explain how communities don't have to be "neighborhoods," but rather groups of belonging with shared identities, values, and goals. The speaker links historical context to intersectional community building.

DISCUSSION QUESTIONS

1. How can Sorrell's frames for understanding be used to critically analyze the communities in which we live, work, and participate?
2. How can the foundational concepts of intercultural communication aid us in any attempts to intervene into "unjust discourses" in order to promote social justice?
3. How do the goals of Communication Action Pedagogy overlap/align with those of intercultural communication?
4. Should/can the intercultural communication classroom be politically neutral? Why/why not?
5. What community partners would benefit from a relationship with an intercultural communication course? Why?

Chapter 6

Deconstructing Ideologies

This book [Afrocentricity: The theory of social change] is written with the idea that an African renaissance is only possible if there is an African ideology, distinct from a Eurocentric ideology, that allows African agency, that is, a sense of self actualizing based upon the best interests of African people. You should sense your power as you read this book and you should know that nothing can replace your own historical location. Find your own center and discover yourself fully.

(Asante, 1980/1998, pp. 1–2)

The imperative of theoretical analysis in a world structured in domination and hierarchy (in particular, class, race, and gender) is primarily ideological: What is communication for? How is communication used to mask the structural violence in the system? What are the sacred ideas used to justify and keep the exploitative system in place? What are the ideology's seduction tactics and strategies? And for that matter, what counts as communication? Who gets to speak? Do other nonhuman beings get to have a say? Does the planet?

(Mendoza, as cited in Alexander, Arasaratnam, Flores et al., 2014, p. 87)

The classroom is not a *neutral* space politically, ideologically, and more. Shor (1993) evokes "education is politics" to suggest that "the entire school experience has political qualities and consequences" (p. 28). Following these sentiments, how might the intercultural communication classroom experience bear political qualities and consequences? Teaching/learning for social justice is a political project that requires considerations of ideologies—visible or hidden—that organize, structure, or orchestrate the intercultural communication classroom.

This chapter reviews and unpacks mutually reinforcing ideologies that have had profound impacts on the study of intercultural communication.

BACKGROUND

How comfortable/uncomfortable do you feel talking about and unpacking ideologies with students? Also, how do you approach conversations about ideology, power, and domination in the classroom? Ideology—a dominant yet often invisible and/or taken-for-granted belief and value system—organizes, structures, and controls how we know what we know. van Dijk (1998) defines ideology succinctly as "the *basis of the social representations shared by members of a group*" (p. 8, emphasis in original). He further explains that "ideologies allow people, as group members, to organize the multitude of social beliefs about what is the case, good or bad, right or wrong, *for them*, and to act accordingly" (van Dijk, 1998, p. 8). Paradoxically, the study of intercultural communication in U.S. academia (starting with the Foreign Service Institute in the 1950s and 1960s) was first necessitated by a set of ideologies that, as the field matures, many scholars have struggled to interrupt and redirect. To teach and learn intercultural communication for social justice requires a critical awareness of how interlocking ideologies influence how we enter, communicate, act, and interact in intercultural situations, how we represent ourselves and cultural Others, and what we believe or not about intercultural communication. While most intercultural communication textbooks might not have a chapter on *ideology*, these taken-for-granted beliefs are the undergirds of common concepts like assimilation, adaptation, immigration, intercultural relationships, and globalization. We argue that conversations about deconstructing ideologies needs to be woven throughout the course.

Among ideologies that have instigated, shaped, informed, and/or constituted the study of intercultural communication, we agree with Holliday (2011) that the ideology of *essentialism* sits "at the centre of common perceptions of culture both in the academy and in everyday life" (p. 4). In brief, essentialism functions to (re)present people's individual choice and behavior as solely and entirely defined and enabled/constrained by their cultures so that "the stereotype becomes the essence of who they are" (Holliday, 2011, p. 4). For instance, operating under an essentialist view of culture based on nationality, people might say things like "People from Taiwan cannot . . . when they arrive in (U.S.) American culture." In a way, the foundation of intercultural communication pedagogy centers around rejecting essentialist and overgeneralized views of cultures to acknowledge and embrace cultural diversities. However, this is easier said than done. Holliday (2011) argues that much work in intercultural communication studies attempts to reject essentialism but "remains neo-essentialist because important essentialist elements are still maintained" (p. 7). This serves as a reminder that deconstructing ideologies is important yet very challenging.

Paradoxically, Anthony Giddens (1979) argues that discursive efforts to control and end one ideology could potentially turn into another form of ideological domination. He states, *"Any type of political discourse, including Marxism, which anticipates an end to ideology, carries thereby the potentiality of becoming itself ideological"* (Giddens, 1979, p. 197, emphasis in original). The challenges of deconstructing ideologies can be understood through the particular ways in which ideologies function and operate in society. Specifically, Giddens (1979) synthesizes three principal ideological forms in society: (a) representing sectional interests (of dominant groups) as universal interests; (b) denying, concealing, or transmuting contradictions; and (c) reifying and naturalizing the status quo, particularly existing social orders, and hierarchies. Mumby (1989) adds the notion of ideological "refraction." *Refraction* refers to the particular way in which light changes direction when passing from one medium to another such as from air to water. In this sense, an ideology (such as "the American Dream") functions like a process of refraction that mobilizes, predisposes, and dictates social actors toward interpreting an event in a certain and specific way. Ultimately, "the crucial question about ideology is not whether it is 'real' or 'false' but how it comes to be believed in and to be lived out" (Loomba, 2005, p. 30). In the next section, we discuss and unpack three intersecting ideologies (e.g., white supremacy, neoliberalism, and U.S. imperialism) that have had profound impacts on the study of intercultural communication.

UNPACKING INTERSECTING IDEOLOGIES

White Supremacy

Together two articles published in 2001 shed light on the intricate and opaque complexities of white supremacy (a.k.a. whiteness) for intercultural communication research and pedagogy. Cooks (2001) offers the critique that early intercultural communication scholarship had been centered on the perspective of providing intercultural training, education, and research to benefit "people who are part of the dominant culture in the United States or who are sojourners and travelers in other countries for a short time" (a.k.a. middle-/upper-class white Americans) (p. 342). In juxtaposition, Martin and Davis (2001) argue that "intercultural communication scholars have rarely explicitly studied the cultural patterns of white people in the United States" (p. 298). These two articles highlight this complex and seemingly contradictory problem in that white supremacy functions to "maintain intercultural communication as about the nonwhite other" only to reproduce whiteness (Nakayama & Martin, 2007, p. 129). For more than two decades, there has been continuous efforts to deconstruct, decenter, and disorient the problem of whiteness or white supremacy in intercultural communication research and pedagogy (see Cooks & Simpson, 2007; McIntosh, Moon, & Nakayama, 2019; Nakayama & Martin, 1999).

Following Allen's (2001) lead, we prefer "(global) white supremacy" to whiteness as a more overly and explicitly political term. As a critical race theorist and Marxist, Allen defines global white supremacy as "the global system that confers unearned power and privilege on those who become identified as white while conferring disprivilege and disempowerment on those who become identified as people of color" (2001, p. 476). This definition better addresses the global and geopolitical system in which intercultural communication operates inside and outside the United States. In short, the globalization of white supremacy depicts a global opportunity structure then and now in which white European ethnics were and are imagined and (re)produced as civilized at the expense of the "uncivilized" persons of color around the globe. As beneficiaries of global white supremacy, "white group membership is based on a shared cognition that actively and necessarily constructs blindness to global white supremacy" (Allen, 2001, p. 481). As an ideology, blindness to and obliviousness of white supremacy is at the heart of how this ideology can universalize white supremacy as humanity, deny contractions, and naturalize white superiority as the status quo (Giddens, 1979). Simpson (2008) echoes that "White supremacy operates both subtly and perniciously within the more complex social or systemic notions of racism" (p. 142).

Within the communication discipline, Nakayama and Krizek's (1995) groundbreaking study theorizes "whiteness as a strategic rhetoric" in that the discursive power and dominant position of whiteness as the universal subject is mapped out and constituted in a set of rhetorical strategies such as defining white negatively, naturalizing white with a scientific definition, and confusing whiteness with nationality (p. 298). Numerous scholars have built and expanded on this trajectory of analyzing white supremacy as a set of rhetorical strategies that uphold and maintain the domination, superiority, and/or invisibility of white cultures and identities (e.g., Griffin, 2015; Moon & Nakayama, 2005; Tierney & Jackson, 2003). For instance, Griffin (2015) extends strategic whiteness from the context of individual rhetoric to media representations by analyzing the 2011 film *The Help*. Consistent with understanding whiteness as rhetorical strategy, Griffin (2015) argues that *The Help* endorses post-racialism—this notion that racism is a thing of the past—to obscure "the strategic labor of whiteness," which functions to (re)center and (re)secure its hegemonic power and dominance (p. 148). Similarly, Tierney and Jackson (2003) deconstruct white supremacy as constituted through a set of three rhetorical fantasy themes: (a) whiteness equals humanity; (b) colorblindness benefits the group in power; and (c) race is deployed by the group in power to cycle notions of Otherness. While it has been a fruitful lens to deconstruct and interrogate white supremacy as rhetorical strategies, at the same time, it would be misleading to think that it is a relatively straightforward task. Nakayama and Krizek (1995) state that "whatever 'whiteness' really means is constituted only through the rhetoric of whiteness. There is no 'true essence' to 'whiteness'; there are only historically contingent constructions of that social location" (p. 293).

For more than two decades since Nakayama and Krizek's (1995) publication, (intercultural) communication research on whiteness has concluded that the subject of whiteness is evasive, unstable, and slippery, and the reproduction of white supremacy remains dynamic, obscure, and sticky. One sticky point, as Carrillo Rowe and Malhotra (2007) articulate, centers on (un)hinging whiteness (as a universalizing and privileging process and pattern) and white identity and/or the white body. How do instructors and students interrogate the reproduction of whiteness as steeped in social, cultural, and everyday practices without (re)centering white identities and bodies? Another sticky point, according to Simpson (2008), is that whiteness morphs and gets in the way of meaningful dialogue across racial lines such as through disguising itself "under the cloak of civility" (p. 151) to police and silence critical voices of those on the margins. Related to the first two, the third sticky point is that the reproduction of white supremacy requires participation, involvement, and consent, whether automatic or involuntary, of both racialized whites and people of color. As Leonardo (2009) puts it, "Whites are the subjects of whiteness, whereas people of color are its objects" (p. 111). Interpellated differentially within the system of white supremacy, whites, Asians, Latinx, Native Americans, Blacks, and mix-raced individuals all negotiate whiteness as a historically, socially, culturally, and politically contingent process and system.

As an ideology, white supremacy is multifaceted and emerges as historically and contextually contingent constructions. Reflecting it as a multifaceted construct, process, and system, Wander, Nakayama, and Martin (1999) use the phrase "beyond whiteness" in an edited collection to refer "to the notion that race cannot be understood apart from class, gender, and sexual orientation" (p. 22). Furthermore, the discursive formations of white supremacy are historically and contextually contingent. For instance, Chen, Simmons, and Kang (2015) identify the manifestation of a dominant ideology at the time under the U.S. Obama presidency with rising post-racial discourses regarding whiteness and racism. They call it "multicultural/multiracial Obama-ism" to describe "a false optimism of racial equity by promoting token celebrations of the multicultural/multiracial experiences while masking racism" (p. 174). Under the U.S. Trump administration, Yep and Lescure (2018) conceptualize *basal whiteness* as "a product of the intersection of White hegemonic masculinity at this historical and political moment with its racist, classist, homophobic, and nationalist overtones and a potential and proclivity toward violence in various symbolic, affective, and material forms" (p. 131). As a discursive and historical process and system, white supremacy can simultaneously elude and contain a reinforcing ideology such as essentialism or colorblindness. At the same time, white supremacy can diffuse, morph, disguise, and remake itself as demanded by a particular context and moment to solidify its power and centrality. It is important to keep all of these in mind when deconstructing, interrogating, and destabilizing this elusive and slippery ideology. For more examples of how intercultural communication scholars have analyzed race, racism, and whiteness, see Moon and Holling's (2016) edited book that features nine chapters originally published in two special issues in the *Journal of International and Intercultural Communication* on race(ing) intercultural communication across U.S. and global contexts.

Western/European/U.S. Imperialism

"Whiteness . . . is often perceived as a synonym for Americanness" (Lea & Sims, 2008, p. 11). As reinforcing ideologies, Western/European/U.S. imperialism relates to and supports white supremacy. Whereas a number of (intercultural) communication scholars have been committed to interrogating and decentering whiteness for more than two decades, less persisting attention has been paid to the deconstruction of Western/European/U.S. imperialism. The guiding question for a 2007 forum published in the flagship journal *Communication Monographs* underscores a need to deconstruct Western/European/U.S. centrism in communication scholarship—"When viewed from standpoints in particular cultures, does mainstream communication theory appear to be culturally biased?" (Craig, 2007, p. 256). The issue forum editor invited four scholars of communication and culture to respond. The consensus is that yes, Eurocentric cultural assumptions and biases limit mainstream communication theory. The fact that the guiding question is framed as a yes/no question as opposed to an open-ended one (e.g., *How are cultural biases perpetuated in mainstream communication theory?*) underscores the power of Eurocentrism in the field of communication. Miike (2006) explains that the communication discipline is "Eurocentric in origin and substance and remain[s] unreflexive on the Eurocentric nature of knowledge" (p. 5). For our purpose, it is useful to consider Eurocentrism and Western and U.S. imperialism together. Even though there are nuances between them, bringing the terms together signals a greater sense of urgency for a more collective response and resistance in the field of (intercultural) communication.

Asante's (1980/1998) Afrocentricity represents one of the earliest efforts to challenge and decenter Western/European/U.S. centrism in communication studies in general and in intercultural communication specifically. Despite it being rooted in communication, Asante's work has been more favorably and enthusiastically embraced in Africana and African American studies. Dr. Asante took his first faculty position in the Department of Communication at Purdue University (1968–1969). However, he has been a professor in the Department of Africology (formerly Department of African American Studies) at Temple University since 1984, including creating the first PhD program in African American Studies in the United States. To what extent might the differing receptions of Professor Asante's Afrocentricity across disciplines signal whether or not deconstructing Western/European/U.S. imperialism is a priority to/in (intercultural) communication scholarship? In juxtaposition to Eurocentric mode of thinking that assumes the human civilization began with the ancient Greeks and Romans (e.g., Socrates, Plato, and Aristotle), Afrocentricity as a philosophical stance starts with and centralizes African agency, interests, values, and worldviews.

At the core of European/Western/U.S. imperialism are the struggles that (formerly) colonized subjects experience in relation to empires and colonial powers that forcibly take over their land and economy, subjugate their historical consciousness, and restructure their sociocultural world in order to fuel imperialist interests. Speaking as a Filipina woman and an international student, Mendoza (2006) describes her struggles coming to the United States as an empire:

> As fate would have it, I was to face Empire no longer from a distance, but up close and personal. My first year of encounter, like round one in a boxing match, left me pretty much reeling and bloodied. When one has grown up under a U.S.-oriented colonial education, with one's imagination completely shaped by that rhetoric of Empire, one does not expect to experience culture shock. After all, had I not been prepared all my life to know America? . . . Yet what does it mean not only to survive the place of your debasement as a colonized subject but to live justly, with healing and forgiveness for the sins of the past? What kind of rapprochement is possible between peoples on opposite sides of the imperial-subject divide? How does a colonized subject make a life for herself in the heart of empire? How does one find the resources to do so? (p. 235)

Domosh (2006) agrees with treating the United States as an empire. Unlike other empires in history built through the power of military takeovers, Domosh contends that the first American empire since the mid-nineteenth century had been built on commercial and economic power, which laid the foundation for the U.S. military interventions of the late nineteenth century and its later economic and cultural domination on the global stage. As an empire, "America's economic imperialism was based primarily on the making and selling of mass-produced commodities" through large American international companies such as H. J. Heinz Company (p. 7). The process of establishing control through free trade and economic integration positioned foreign peoples and nations as consumers and also as feminized/*other*ed subjects in relation to the United States as the masculine producer. The struggles, problematics, and contexts of colonization and decolonization describe postcolonial studies as an interdisciplinary field of inquiry and critique.

Postcolonial studies represents another response to European/Western/U.S. imperialism. Shome and Hegde (2002) first introduced postcolonial approaches to communication. Echoing concerns of Eurocentric biases in the communication discipline (e.g., Craig, 2007), Shome and Hegde (2002) urge:

> If theory in communication is to reflect the exigencies of the global moment then we need to rethink the ways in which our intellectual quest relates to the cultural and social formations around us.... Denaturalizing communication (to use Grossberg's words) and problematizing culture from a postcolonial perspective allows us to go beyond the descriptive and account for the ways in which the Western realities have spread across the world as the universal condition. (pp. 260–261)

To Shome and Hegde (2002), postcolonial studies is distinct from other areas of critical scholarship in that "postcolonial scholarship provides a historical and international depth to the understanding of cultural power" in ways that extend beyond the nation-state and theorize cultural conditions of contemporary society (p. 252). This distinctiveness is not only consistent with the goals of (critical) intercultural communication scholarship but also extends its reach.

Building on Afrocentricity, Asiacentricity represents still another response to European/Western/U.S. imperialism. Miike (2006) describes Asiacentricity as "a way of understanding the commonality *and* complexity of the Asian experience through Asian languages, religious-philosophical traditions, and historical struggles as vital resources for theory building" (p. 16, emphasis in original). From this lens, Miike (2007) identifies five key biases of communication theory as a Western and Eurocentric field: (a) individuality and independence bias; (b) ego-centeredness and self-enhancement bias; (c) reason and rationality bias; (d) rights and freedom bias; and (e) pragmatism and materialism bias.

Conversations about Western/European/U.S. imperialism should not be limited to the subfield of intercultural communication considering that this challenge/problematic/issue is steeped across the entire communication discipline. While white supremacy and Western/European/U.S. imperialism are mutually reinforcing ideologies, we the authors call for more systematic efforts to address Eurocentrism and U.S. imperialism specifically in our research and pedagogy. Consistent with the trends in the field, our research also found that more critical intercultural communication teachers have been challenging and unpacking white supremacy in their classes and fewer are addressing U.S. imperialism specifically (Chen & Lawless, 2019).

Neoliberalism

Neoliberalism—the universalization, extension, and dissemination of market values and enterprise logic to all institutions and social actions—has restructured and corporatized higher education. Kwitonda (2017) synthesizes four lines of thinking about neoliberalism (a) as an ideological hegemonic project, (b) as policy and program, (c) as state form, and (d) as governmentality. Within higher education, neoliberalism works to neutralize critical contexts and obscure social injustices through privileging revenues, naturalizing competitions, promoting individualism, redefining teacher-student relations through the lens of consumerism, and commodifying education (Kahl, 2018). Thus, institutions of higher education become neoliberal universities.

Neoliberalism is of relevance to intercultural communication scholarship. In analyzing an ambivalent relationship between neoliberalism and nationalism in the case of Japan, Kawai (2009) points out that "neoliberalism is problematic for intercultural communication since it makes power relations invisible and contexts intangible, thereby making better intercultural communication with others difficult" (p. 34). Related, neoliberalism has restructured conversations about cultures and diversities to be more about consumption and commodification than about critical thinking and learning. For instance, building on research indicating that "diversity" is mostly framed through a neoliberal lens in (U.S.) higher education (e.g., Ahmed, 2007), Ashby-King and Hanasono (2019) found in their study that "approximately 97% of participants communicated diversity as a celebration of individual differences and a mechanism for inclusivity and community" (p. 6). They surveyed 116 undergraduate communication students at a predominantly white Midwestern university asking them to respond to this open-ended prompt, "How do *you* define diversity?" Their findings evidence the power of neoliberalism in the (U.S.) academy as well as the need for critical conversations about "diversity" as it intersects with unequal systems of power, privilege, and oppression. In particular, this study underscores the role that students play while nudging instructors to lead and facilitate such conversations.

In addition, neoliberalism has filtered and framed discourse of multiculturalism in ways that cheapen, commodify, and render dispensable individuals and groups that multicultural discourses are supposed to serve. Darder

(2012) defines *neoliberal multiculturalism* as the "acknowledgement and acceptance of multicultural subjects, based on an ethos of self-reliance, individualism, competition, while simultaneously (and conveniently) undermining discourses and social practices that call for collective social action and fundamental social change" (p. 417). In our analysis of the experiences of immigrant women faculty in U.S. academia through the lens of neoliberalism multiculturalism, we call for rethinking the ways which "diversity," "multiculturalism," and "internationalization" are treated, discussed, and practiced on many U.S. colleges and universities (Lawless & Chen, 2017).

KEY CHALLENGES

One challenge to deconstructing ideologies with students is a growing yet problematic assumption that the classroom should be *neutral* as U.S. society becomes increasingly polarized and divisive. As a microcosm of society, the classroom is an inherently political terrain. Under the Trump administration, many instructors and colleagues we know feel less safe and more vulnerable talking about ideologies such as white supremacy with their students. Of course, feeling safe itself is a form of privilege that has been and continues to be denied to instructors belonging to certain groups such as those who are undocumented, Muslim (American) women, and more. Also, the exercise of deconstructing ideologies can easily turn into counterproductive conversations of waging ideological wars when students confuse value systems with taken-for-granted beliefs. Carefully articulating the notion of "taken-for-granted" beliefs can help students deconstruct their own value systems. Asking students to think of *where* and *when* they came to hold a particular belief helps to elucidate structures of socialization (e.g., family, religious institutions, peers, schools, media). We call this chapter "deconstructing ideologies" because we firmly believe in a process of not just talking about ideologies, but helping students to break them down and determine how they were socially formulated and bolstered over time. Deconstructing ideologies is a dynamic process of learning to become aware of ideas, tensions, and contradictions that instructors and students have been socialized not to see, think about, or discuss. It can also be a stressful process of unlearning socialization practices that have conditioned us to see, feel, and think about the self, the world, and others in particular ways.

Another challenge is that deconstructing ideologies such as white supremacy can trigger a wide range of emotions (e.g., anxiety, guilt, fragility, resentment, frustration, trauma). Sometimes students might not realize that they are triggered or are triggering others in the classroom. Finding a text that students can relate to can be very helpful. For conversations about deconstructing white supremacy, we have found Warren's (2010) article, "It Really Isn't about You: Whiteness and the Dangers of Thinking You Got It," to be one such relatable and engaging text.

STORIES FROM THE FIELD

Godfried Asante, San Diego State University

As critical intercultural communication instructors, deconstructing particular racial ideologies with students such as whiteness comes with challenges because of the deeply intertwined notion of liberal humanism and whiteness. Students who occupy multiple intersections of privileges with regard to race, gender, class, sexuality, ability, religion, among others, tend to have an unwavering belief in the rational human subject as the unproblematic harbinger of social progress. This unyielding belief in the individual is a myth propagated by whiteness. As such, it is essential to draw their attention to how such ideologies can be dangerous, especially for people of color. The story below derives from my intercultural communication class, where students presented the issue of skin bleaching in West Africa.

As a group research project, students presented one of my articles—"Glocalized Whiteness": Sustaining and Reproducing Whiteness through Skin Toning in Ghana. This article engages with the predominance of skin bleaching as practiced across West Africa and seeks to provide an alternative reason to why women especially bleach their skin even though skin bleaching creams are banned across many parts in Africa. Skin bleaching is the material consequence of the European conquest of the non-white world. Largely produced and distributed by European and U.S. American corporations such as L'Oréal, Proctor and Gamble, Unilever, Johnson & Johnson, among several others, skin bleaching products are used to "correct" Blackness. During the Q&A, half of the class mentioned that skin bleaching is the same as skin tanning as it is practiced in the West. I stated that both skin tanning and skin bleaching are similar in practice but the material conditions and sociopolitical contexts influencing both practices are different. According to one student, concerning women who bleach or tan, whether they are based in the United States or Ghana is irrelevant because they are making individual choices based on their class positions. As such, skin bleaching is not influenced by racial ideologies of anti-Blackness but by class positioning only.

In response, I asked students to think about the colonial histories that have produced both nations—the United States and Ghana—and how those histories have produced different variations of the "individual rational subject." I noted that given the historical context of colonialism, economic disenfranchisement, and heteropatriarchy, women who bleach their skin do it as a form of survival. Conversely, skin tanning is not borne out of the need to survive.

In order to help them develop critical thinking, I asked students to research the colonial histories and the contemporary iterations of social disparities that may have produced and continue to generate barriers that disproportionally displace racial minorities and nonwestern subjects from achieving self-determination and empowerment. For the next class, the conversation had shifted from emphasizing the women's individual choice to bleach to the institutional and structural barriers that influence the practice. Exploring the historical context of colonialism and imperialism and how it influences the present was crucial to the disruption of the "individual rational subject" as universal standards for exploring social issues on a global scale.

Dr. Asante's activity is useful as a pedagogical tool for deconstructing ideologies, and also because it exemplifies ways in which educators can respond to students' understanding in the moment. The activity outlined here was a response to students (mis)understandings as they surfaced in the classroom. As a result, the conversation about ideologies continued, deepened, and ultimately led to more informed and critically thinking students.

PEDAGOGICAL ACTIVITIES

Re-learning American History

This published activity (McNabb & Friedman, 2009) asks students to challenge their assumptions about cultures other than their own by researching the histories they never learned in school. Moreover, students are asked to think critically about why a particular group's history has been systematically left out of U.S. history classes. Students should gain a better understanding of how ideologies about the "other" are constructed and maintained through systematic erasure of histories in lieu of a dominant cultural narrative.

"Are You Upholding White Supremacy?" (Lopez Bunyasi & Smith, 2019, pp. 145–166)

In this book chapter, Lopez Bunyasi and Smith (2019) highlight and unpack some of the scripts that many of us have learned, which inadvertently uphold white supremacy. In their book, *Stay Woke: A People's Guide to Making All Black Lives Matter*, white supremacy is defined as: "1. The systemic provision of political, social, economic, and psychological benefits and advantages to white. . . . 2. A set of norms and expectations predicated on white habitus, or the preferences, tastes, emotions, and perceptions of white Americans. 3. The belief that white people are inherently superior to people of color and should dominate over people of color" (2019, p. 113). They unpack and challenge the problematics of common scripts such as "It doesn't matter if you're

Black or white or green or blue!"; "I voted for Obama"; and "I did not vote for Trump" that allows folks to remain "good, friendly complicit racists" (p. 147). This is an accessible chapter to assign and talk through the structural and ideological system of white supremacy.

Theatre of the Oppressed

Rowe, Rudnick, and White (2019) have developed a two-stage activity utilizing Augusto Boal's Theater of the Oppressed methods (i.e., stage one of sculptures of the self and stage two of rainbow of desire installation). The goal of this activity is to engage in reflexivity through exploring nuances of power and identity nonverbally and aesthetically.

Decoding Popular Culture

This assignment (embedded in Appendix G) asks students to conduct an analysis of a popular text (e.g., movie, TV show, commercial music video, book, political campaign) and present a dominant, negotiated, and oppositional reading of the text. Students practice deconstructing ideologies within larger narratives and present their findings to the class.

VIDEOS AS TEACHING TOOLS

Layla F. Saad—the author of *Me and White Supremacy*—is interviewed about her book—a twenty-eight-day journey that challenges individuals to reflect upon harmful ideologies and deconstruct white supremacy, complicity, and social justice.

Capitalism and the American Dream Are a Myth—In this Now What video, Denise Hearn explains why capitalism is a harmful ideology that perpetuates disadvantage and concentrates wealth. This explanation can supplement discussions about the American Dream as a myth.

DISCUSSION QUESTIONS

1. Is the American Dream a myth? Why/why not?
2. How can we become aware of the ideologies that we subscribe to?
3. How do the ideologies that we subscribe to influence our choices and actions on a daily basis?
4. Can there be positive ideologies? How would they operate?
5. How do ideologies become "taken-for-granted"?

Chapter 7

Thinking and Acting Globally

To globalize the study of communication is to continually produce a resistant body of knowledge about the vectors that connect and disconnect culture, space, and inevitably power.

(Shome & Hegde, 2002, p. 188)

In the context of globalization, our choices and actions are always enabled, shaped, and constrained by history, relations of power, and material conditions that are inextricably linked to intercultural dimensions of culture, race, class, religion, sexual orientation, language, and nationality.

(Sorrells, 2010, p. 184)

Globalization as a new world state not only connects people but also dislocates them.

(Atay, 2015, p. 21)

Writing this chapter in the midst of a *global* pandemic due to the spread of COVID-19 (novel coronavirus disease-2019) is a challenging experience in unprecedented ways, which is also an unusual opportunity to (re)consider how to live, think, and act in this world. We are still grappling with how this pandemic is global in scale, reach, and consequences. Personally, when the pandemic was first reported in January 2020, Yea-Wen was more worried about her families in Taiwan and Japan than her immigrant family of three in San Diego, California. However, as the pandemic came under control in Taiwan but COVID-19 cases and deaths sharply rose in the United States in April 2020, Yea-Wen relied on her mother to physically *mail* her face masks made in Taiwan. Writing this chapter through the pandemic has highlighted for us the evolving forces, complexities, and struggles of globalization as well as responses to it. When drafting this chapter in early 2020, countries around the world began to witness an unprecedented spread of a new strain of a novel coronavirus named SARS-COV-2 since its first reporting to the WHO (World Health Organization) Country office in China on December 31, 2019. On January 30, 2020, the WHO declared the outbreak a "Public Health Emergency of International Concern." Except for countries neighboring China, most of the Western societies did not take this virus or disease seriously despite warning signs. As of March 5, 2020, there were 95,265 reported cases of COVID-19 with 3,281 deaths across thirty-four countries (World Health Organization, 2020). Among them, 80% of the cases were found in three countries: China, South Korea, and Italy. Around that time, Brandi ended up canceling her trip traveling from San Francisco to write with Yea-Wen in San Diego. Shortly for us in California, Governor Gavin Newsom ordered all Californians to stay home in order to curb potential community spread of COVID-19, prevent hospitals from becoming overwhelmed, and save lives. Following the lead of other countries, many governors across the United States made their own versions of stay-at-home orders in March and April 2020. For both of us as academic parents, this meant the beginning of working and teaching from home with our respective children: a toddler for Brandi and a kindergartener for Yea-Wen. (At least, we still have our jobs when countless across the globe have lost theirs.) As of May 15, there were 1,443,245 COVID-19 cases and 25,050 deaths reported in the United States alone (National Public Radio, 2020). During the months of March and April 2020, the United States had reported some of the highest numbers of COVID-19 cases than any other countries. Like interruptions in many sectors and industries across countries due to COVID-19 (e.g., airlines, hotels, restaurants, retail shop, and more), the writing of this particular chapter was disrupted for nearly two months. During this ongoing global pandemic, the world as we knew it shifted and the world as we know it is still shifting. As painful as they could be, ruptures and disruptions are also rich moments for critical reflections and reevaluations in this case about forces, tensions, and struggles of globalization. We concur with Appadurai (1996) that the central force and struggle of globalization is "the tension between cultural homogenization and cultural heterogenization" (p. 32). Following Shome and Hegde (2002), we approach globalization as "a process and a phenomenon that is always hard at work, as it were . . . and it relies on several overlapping structures and relations, from the local, to the national, to the global" (p. 175).

Teaching/learning for social justice is inherently a global project. The increasing forces, conditions, and processes of globalization today mandate a need to think and act both locally and globally. Chapter 6 reviews literature on cultural dimensions of globalization and enacting intercultural praxis as global citizenship. Grounded in this body of literature, we will discuss teaching/learning tools and activities that promote intercultural citizenship.

BACKGROUND

McLuhan first introduced the idea of a "global village" in his 1962 book, *The Gutenberg Galaxy: The Making of Typographic Man*, to highlight the development and acceleration of the "new electronic interdependence" recreating the world as a global village (McLuhan, 2011, p. 36). Departing from this image of a global village, Appadurai (1996) depicts the ruptured landscapes of globalization as *imagined worlds*—extending Anderson's (1983) approach to nations as imagined communities—in that "the multiple worlds that are constituted by the historically situated imaginations of persons and groups spread around the globe" (p. 33). Unlike scholars like McLuhan who celebrate increasing global interdependence and interconnectivity, (critical) intercultural communication scholars voice and share concerns about the challenges, problematics, and struggles of globalization especially those who are on the margins and peripheries of societies. In contrast to McLuhan's interdependent, connected, and uniform "global village," Shome and Hegde (2002) highlight a core assumption about globalization in that unequal and uneven flows of capitals and cultural images across the globe produce "relations of disjunctures (and conjectures)" (p. 174). Further, Shome and Hegde argue that, under the disguise of globalization as "a universal, all-inclusive concept" (2002, p. 181), globalization as a process and phenomenon can (re)produce existing configurations of power and hierarchies of otherness. Similarly, Sorrells (2010) defines globalization as a "complex web of economic, political, and technological forces that have brought people, cultures, cultural products, and markets, as well as beliefs, practices and ideologies into increasingly greater proximity to and con/disjunction with one another within inequitable relations of power" (p. 171). This definition signals Sorrells's approach to globalization with an emphasis on the global contexts, conditions, and processes that are simultaneously cultural, political, economic, and more.

Globalization is a multidimensional, complex, interlayered, and increasingly more contested phenomenon. In Appadurai's (1996) analysis of the cultural dimensions of globalizations as imagined worlds, five dimensions of the global cultural flower are identified and discussed: (a) ethnoscapes, (b) technoscapes, (c) financescapes, (d) mediascapes, and (e) ideoscapes. The suffix -*scape* highlights the fluid and irregular shapes of these five global landscapes: (a) *ethnoscapes* refer to persons who constitute the shifting world we live (e.g., tourists, immigrants whether documented or undocumented, refugees, guest workers, asylum seekers, and more); (b) *techscapes* describe technology whether high or low and mechanical or informational; (c) *financescapes* address the increasingly rapid and mysterious disposition of global capitals; (b) *mediascapes* refer to images produced and distributed by traditional and new media such as newspapers, magazines, television stations, film studies, and social networking sites) to disseminate information; and (e) *ideoscapes* focus on concatenations of political images dealing with the ideologies of states and the counter-ideologies of movements. Similar to Appadurai's framework, intercultural communication scholars studying globalization tend to focus on the cultural aspects of the globalization processes as they intersect with historical, geopolitical, and economic forces. For instance, Atay (2015) offers a cyber-ethnography examining cultural identity formations of diasporic queer bodies in queer spaces. Rooted in critical intercultural communication, Toyosaki and Eguchi's (2017) edited collection examines homogenizing discursive systems of cultural identities such as performative accomplishments in and about Japan. In her book organized by a globalization framework, Sorrells (2016) unpacks three interrelated facets of globalization: (a) intercultural dimensions of economic globalization, (b) intercultural dimensions of political globalization, and (c) intercultural dimensions of cultural globalization.

To critical intercultural communication scholars, the genesis of globalization is understood as beginning in 1492 with the voyage of Columbus across the Atlantic that marks the start of European and territorial colonialism and imperialism. The first wave of globalization was set in motion in 1492, which gave profound meaning to skin color differentiating the colonizer versus the colonized. Since then, the underlying forces of racism and white supremacy have continued and persisted. Over the next 500 years or so, the social machine of racism and white supremacy has only evolved to be more complex, interwoven, and interlocking with other systems of oppression based on gender, class, and more. Thus, globalization as we understand and experience it today can be understood as a new phase of cultural imperialism and colonization (a.k.a. colonialization 2.0 or 3.0). Speaking of the historical, cultural, and political significance of 1492, Rodríguez (2018) states as a woman of color (raised in El Salvador) in response to being advised to act as white: "I never belonged, because that's a category [white] that was imagined by colonizers and reframed and reworked and redefined throughout the centuries since 1492" (p. 43). Even though cultural traditions and practices have adapted and evolved with time, inequities rooted in cultural hierarchies such as based on race have remained. To what extent have equity gaps increased and widened as forces and processes of globalization continue? Further, Asante (2016) reminds us that globalization is a dual and mutually reinforcing process of globalizing and localizing at the same time. Asante theorizes the concept of "glocalized whiteness" to illustrate this mode of thinking. In short, glocalized whiteness illustrates this dual process of distancing "from the general conception of whiteness yet constituted locally to reflect the naturalizing and normalizing process of white-supremacist social order" (Asante, 2016, p. 90).

Even though migration is central to an increasingly globalized world, intercultural communication scholars have paid scant attention to the cultural politics of (im)migration until recently. Ono (1998) has critiqued the inertia among intercultural communication scholars at the time to take nationalistic approaches; instead, he argues for a need to problematize "nation" and focus on lived intercultural experiences. The nationalistic focus in early intercultural communication research has directed attention away from the in-between spaces and the mobile manners in which (im)migrants occupy and live. Flores (2003) evidences competing and complementary narratives of immigration that frame Mexican immigrants and bodies as foreign, distasteful, and ambivalently desirable and also construct rhetorical borders positioning them on the outside of U.S. American-ness. Shome (2003) further complicates the in-between spaces that (im)migrants live by highlighting an unnamed place or space for undocumented immigrants. She states, "Many immigrants caught in the transnational relations of space in the border are, in many cases, unable to become diasporic in that they are unable to cross over to the 'other side'" (Shome, 2003, p. 53). Cheng (2008) examines the lived experiences of transnational Taiwanese and Chinese immigrants operating maquiladoras—assembly factories—on the U.S.-Mexico border, which underscores the importance, if not imperative, of analyzing how cultures and identities are communicated from multiple fronts. Similarly, we ourselves have examined the lived negotiations of immigrant women faculty in U.S. academia to unpack how women across race, class, and immigration status differentially negotiate the politics of white supremacy, multicultural neoliberalism, paradox of assimilation, and more (e.g., Chen, 2018; Chen & Lawless, 2018; Lawless & Chen, 2017). Eguchi (2011) reminds us that (im)migrant bodies are not just racialized but also sexualized in ways that complicate their intersecting positions as cultural Others.

Among the intersecting forces of globalization (e.g., global capitalism, migration, climate change, media, and popular culture), intercultural communication scholars have paid particular attention to new media since the early 2010s. Chen (2012) highlights the thinking behind it when he states: "The rapid development of new media has been the main force accelerating the trend of globalization in human society in recent decades. New media has brought human integration and society to a highly interconnected and complex level, but at the same time challenges the very existence of intercultural communication in its traditional sense" (p. 1). Shuter (2012) argues that new media is the new frontier in intercultural communication studies and refers to this new field of inquiry as "intercultural new media studies." Since the early 2010s, intercultural communication scholars have been grappling with how technological and media advancements (e.g., Skype, Facebook, Twitter, Snapchat, and Instagram) (re)shape intercultural encounters, interactions, and relationships. The global pandemic of COVID-19 has further accelerated and taken this trend to the next level with a sudden and drastic push for distance learning and online instruction via Zoom and more. One particular example stands out to us. When COVID-19 forced schools and universities to cancel in-person commencements, a group of students and alumni at University of California, Berkeley, innovated and coordinated with university officials to host its 2020 commencement on Minecraft, a virtual gaming platform, under the name of Blockeley University: https://www.blockeley.com/. This initiative originated with students and was carried out and successfully executed by students and alumni. This example does not just speak to the power of new media but also the instrumental and crucial role that students play. The latter (a.k.a. students) often do not get enough recognition and acknowledgment that they deserve.

So, how might new media impact the study of intercultural communication? Shuter (2012) identifies new media and intercultural communication theory as a primary area of study and culture and new media as secondary area. Building on existing research, Shuter specifies three particular directions for linking new media and intercultural communication theory: (a) cultural identities (e.g., hybrid cultural identities in virtual communities); (b) intercultural dialogue and third culture; and (c) acculturation and intercultural competence. Considering the characteristics of new media (i.e., digitality, convergency, interactivity, hypertextuality, and virtuality), Chen (2012) identifies three topical areas to investigate the impact of new media on intercultural communication: (a) how national/ethnic cultures impact the development of new media; (b) how new media impact cultural/social identities; and (c) how new media, especially social media, impact different aspects of intercultural interactions such as intercultural relationships, intercultural dialogue, and intercultural conflicts. One direction that has received less discussion is how new media might contribute to widen and enlarge existing social gaps within, among, and across cultural groups.

ENACTING INTERCULTURAL PRAXIS AS GLOBAL CITIZENSHIP

I think my best moment [when teaching Intercultural Communication] is taking students out of the classroom and taking them to the XXX center for Peace and Justice, and one student was like, "Oh I didn't even know this place existed." . . . Like maybe in my classroom I can just talk about it. I can brush it off. But when I'm in a non-classroom space dealing with some sort of community issue, I can't run away. I'm there.

This is a quote from one of the twenty intercultural communication instructors we interviewed for the research project that informs this book. It underscores that praxis-based social justice is at the heart of critical intercultural communication pedagogy. At the same time, praxis-based pedagogy is messy and becomes contradictory within marketplace universities. Another participant in our study, a white/woman/assistant professor spoke to this messiness when she discussed what went into engagement in social justice activism: "the risk taking, the embodiment, the awareness of when you're doing something stupid and the ability to call yourself out on that." In this section, we highlight enacting intercultural praxis as a useful lens to consider thinking and acting globally and locally.

We as citizens of a global community are becoming more interconnected in unprecedented ways, and many of the issues and problems (such as global warming and fair trade) that we face today require coordinated efforts and commitments from leaders, organizers, and citizens across countries. *Citizenship* entails allegiance, rights, and responsibilities as a citizen, community, belonging, and more. In the context of an increasingly globalized world, what does being a citizen of the world today mean, and who decides? Drawing on the experiences of (highly skilled and privileged) transnational Chinese with mobility, flexibility, and citizenship, Ong (1999) conceptualizes *flexible citizenship* as "the strategies and effects of mobile mangers, technocrats, and professionals seeking to both circumvent *and* benefit from different nation-state regimes by selecting different sites for investments, work, and family relocation" (p. 112). In contrast, how about citizenship for the undocumented, the dislocated, and the migrant children separated from their families?

Drawing on Paulo Freire's critical pedagogy and praxis that links theory, research, and practice, Sorrells and Nakagawa (2008) discuss and develop *intercultural praxis* as "critique, action and intervention" (p. 34). In brief, intercultural communication praxis offers a critical and reflective process of being, thinking, feeling, and acting in an increasingly globalized world as an ethical intercultural communicator for social and global justice. Sorrells's (2016) framework of intercultural praxis has six interwoven entry points: inquiry, framing, positioning, dialogue, reflection, and action. *Inquiry* refers to a willingness and desire to know, ask, and learn about both the self and cultural Others. *Framing* focuses on a range of perspective-taking lenses, tools, and options in intercultural praxis. *Positioning* considers the socially constructed categories of difference and power that position us always already in relation to Others. *Dialogue* invites each person to stretch, expand, and (re)imagine the self by first surrendering to the Other. *Reflection* describes a growth mindset and capacity to learn from introspection, observation, and (re)consideration. *Action* joins increased understanding with responsible action striving to make a difference in the world. Similarly, Collier (2014) develops a framework of "critical/interpretive praxis" in community engagement for working with cultural communities across the globe. Her book features cases of intercultural dances across differences with community-based organizations in Nepal, Northern Ireland, Zimbabwe, Kenya, and the United States. In particular, Collier offers a series of key considerations to move through the framework of critical/interpretive praxis: (a) consider the organizations, work, and dances with communities; (b) dance with reflexivity asking why and how researcher/practitioner position matter; (c) dance with contexts and structures of community engagement; (d) consider spaces and places of community engagement and dances with difference; (e) negotiate cultural identifications, representations, and positions; (f) dance with difference in relationships and relations; and (g) consider what the community engagement work accomplishes.

COVID-19 reaffirms for us that the heart of our pedagogy lies in our loyalty and commitment to our students. We cannot teach students to solve problems in the future that we cannot anticipate today. As forces of globalization and localization continue to shift and morph the world, what we think we can offer are tools, skills, and practices that promote social justice in thinking and acting globally.

KEY CHALLENGES FOR GLOBAL CITIZENSHIP AND ENGAGEMENT

Challenging capitalist ideologies in a capitalistic society like the United States can be met with conscious and unconscious resistance. Further, in resistance to global capitalism, what might it look like to develop a cultural self through cultivating an ability to problematize and critique oneself? Talking about global citizenship and engagement requires moving beyond the notion that we should only think of ourselves and challenges strongly held individualistic tendencies (e.g., "American first"). Such a mindset distracts from promoting a sense of global belonging and citizenship. In addition, patriotism that feeds and is fed by nationalism as a response to globalization poses challenges for conversations about thinking globally and acting locally. For instance, could anti-globalization thinking serve as a productive way of thinking globally and acting locally?

Figuring out concrete ways to see and engage in processing the intimate and intricate connections between the local and the global can be challenging. If students are not invested in or are skeptical of the idea of global citizenship and engagement to start with, how can you have meaningful conversations about the connections between the local and the global? Moreover, when conversations about globalization become heated in the classroom, how can you ensure that students from marginalized positions such as refugees and undocumented immigrants do not become wounded or harmed?

Students can overcome these hurdles by thinking about the ways they are connected to global Others. Ask students to contemplate, "How is my well-being wrapped up in the well-being of global Others?" When using a human rights or social justice framework, students begin to see their livelihood connected to those across the globe. Moreover, this exercise promotes empathy for the human condition. The activities described in the following can help students to think through these connections.

STORIES FROM THE FIELD

Kathryn Sorrells—California State University, Northridge

You've likely heard the phrase "Think globally, act locally." Popularized in the 1970s and 1980s as environmental movements gained momentum around the world, the concept behind the slogan germinated in grassroots organizing dating back to the early 1900s by a Scottish urban planner and activist. This prescient call takes on new and more urgent meanings today as we experience multiple pandemics—a global environmental crisis, a global public health crisis, and a global crisis of racialized state violence—and as we struggle forward toward a safer, healthier, more equitable and just world.

While nuanced and used differently in different situations, the phrase, "Think globally, act locally," underscores the relationship between what is happening in a particular location—wherever one is—and what is occurring in broader environments. Initially, a century and a quarter ago, the emphasis was on immediate environments in proximity to and surrounding the primary location. The twentieth century with two world wars, on-going anti-colonial and de-colonial movements, the formation of international bodies of governance, and the first images of Earth from the moon in 1969, all contributed to shifting perspectives and consciousness toward international interconnectedness and interrelationships. In the past thirty years, advanced communication and transportation technologies along with neoliberal economic and political policies have materially and rhetorically produced a "globalized" world, albeit with highly uneven benefit and impact. And now, the urgency of the environmental crisis for the entire planet, the ravages of Covid-19 pandemic, and the resolute refrain of the Black Lives Matter movement reverberating around the globe from Minneapolis to Atlanta to Los Angeles, and from Palestine to England to South Africa have elevated a stark view and embodied experience of our global interdependence, our persistent inequities, and our uneven precarities.

While "Think globally, act locally" is a spatial concept, it also has temporal relationships embedded within it. The linkage of histories that have created inequities across the globe—ranging from slavery to colonization to neoliberal capitalism—with the present are critical to address. Understanding the Black Lives Matter movement necessitates recognizing the history of white supremacy, slavery, Jim Crow, mass incarceration, and police brutality that have spanned continents and centuries.

"Thinking and acting g(locally)," a 2020 revision of the phrase, insists we see, understand, and act with an awareness of the linkages across place and time of colonial/imperial oppressive forces and of people's struggles for liberation and humanity against these very forces. "Thinking and acting g(locally)" calls on us to ask questions that travel beyond our immediate environments, pull the threads of connection that are historically rooted, attend to the ties that bind what is happening here with what is occurring around the globe, and to act locally with a consciousness of global interconnection and solidarity. As symbols of colonialism, racism, and white supremacy—statues of Robert E. Lee and Christopher Columbus—topple in the United States, so too, monuments to slave traders in England, colonial kings in Belgium, and British military in New Zealand come down. As Black Lives Matter organizers, partners, and allies take to the streets in the United States against police brutality, Palestinians stand in solidary against racialized state-sanctioned violence in the United States And at the same time, Palestinians and global allies rise up against the latest annexation plan and Israeli apartheid under President Trump's "vision for peace" for the region.

What are the connections? What are the linkages between disproportionate targeting, killing, and incarceration of Black and Brown people by police in the U.S. and Israeli occupation and annexation of Palestine? How is racialized state-sanctioned violence integral to capitalism—from plantation capitalism in the colonial period to neoliberal racial capitalism today?

"Thinking and acting g(locally)" means we are conscious of the linkages between the global and the local—historically and today. It means we act here and now with a multi-dimensional focus linking "here" with "there" and "now" with both the "past" and "future." Beyond toppling historical monuments, we must dismantle institutions, practices, and mindsets that sustain racialized state violence, white supremacy, and neoliberal capitalism. "Thinking and acting g(locally)" is critical to envisioning and enacting relationships, institutions, practices, and mindsets rooted in non-violence, decoloniality, equity, and justice.

Reflecting increasing yet uneven interlinkages between the global and the local, Dr. Sorrells's story revisits the popular phrase "Think globally, act locally" and offers a 2020 revision of the phrase as "Thinking and acting g(locally)." Her story reminds us that globalization and glocalization are not just spatial but also temporal/historical concepts, and urges us to think and act seriously about how and why certain disproportionate inequalities such as racism persist across space, time, and history. "Thinking and acting g(locally)" engages us in envisioning and enacting intercultural communication differently toward non-violence, equity, and justice.

PEDAGOGICAL ACTIVITIES

In addition to the reflective practices suggested earlier, we offer several activities that can guide discussion on thinking and acting globally.

Mapping Your Consumption

In this published activity (Kuehl & Hungerford, 2017), students document the production originals of their personal belongings. Students then research the context of globalization in one or more of the countries on their list and discuss the ethical implications of consumption.

"The Phone at the End of the World"

In this published activity (Kerber, 2020), students analyze various arguments on globalization through engaging with Episode 755 titled "The Phone at the End of the World" of *Planet Money*, a National Public Radio podcast. This episode features Argentina's experiment with economic policies aimed at "undoing" globalization, which provides a rich opportunity to engage students in debating various arguments on the promises and pitfalls of globalization.

Stories of Migration

Assign students individually or as a small group to reach out to one individual who has migrated to the United States and to conduct an interview whether face-to-face or virtually. Then, ask students to reflect on the interview discourse either in the form of a reflection essay and/or an oral presentation. This activity deploys lived stories to engage students in thinking about the dynamics and/or conditions of globalization.

Researching Refugee Olympic Team (2016/2020)

The first Refugee Olympic Team was created and competed in the Olympic Games at Rio in 2016: https://www.olympic.org/refugee-olympic-team. A Refugee Olympic Team will continue in the Olympic Games Tokyo 2021. Assign students to research the Refugee Olympic Team and competing athletes to better understand globalization from the standpoint of refugees.

"We're a Culture, Not a Costume" Poster Campaign (2011)

Simmons (2014) conducts an ethical analysis examining and identifying dilemmas around a 2011 post campaign, "We're a Culture, Not a Costume," orchestrated by Ohio University's Students Teaching About Racism in Society (S*T*A*R*S): https://www.ohio.edu/orgs/stars/Poster_Campaign.html. Following Simmons's lead, engage students in applying an intercultural praxis framework to analyze and unpack this poster campaign.

Intercultural Praxis Paper

This assignment (embedded in Appendix G) aims to develop students' awareness of their own intercultural interactions and experiences. As a critical self-assessment, the assignment asks students to assess their own strengths and weaknesses with regard to ethical and socially just intercultural communication. An emphasis can be added to encourage an assessment of global/local interactions, privilege/oppressions related to globalization, and participation in the consumption/appropriation of culture.

VIDEOS AS TEACHING TOOLS

Harvest of Empire: The Untold Story of Latinos in America: This film explores U.S. intervention into Latin American policy and subsequent immigration from a variety of Latin American countries to the United States. The film is useful in demonstrating how globalization impacts economic and national policy, and subsequently, migration.

Crash Course: *Globalization I: The Upside* and *Globalization II: Good or Bad?*: These videos are short supplements for a discussion of globalization that help define the concept, introduce economic interdependence, and weigh the pros and cons of globalization.

DISCUSSION QUESTIONS

1. How have you personally been affected by globalization?
2. How is globalization a positive force? For whom?
3. How is globalization a destructive force? For whom?
4. How has globalization changed the way we study intercultural communication?
5. What ideologies have influenced the spread of globalization?
6. How do you imagine the ongoing forces of globalization affecting our intercultural communication twenty years from now?

Chapter 8

"Assessing" Intercultural Pedagogies for Social Justice

> *Although critical debates over assessment and the neoliberal takeover of education continue—and they should, in my view—university faculty and administrators are facing pressures from institutions outside of higher education, such as funding bodies and businesses, to provide data on student-learning outcomes. Assessment experts from other disciplines are becoming involved in this process. These experts are not necessarily familiar with the content or history of the communication discipline. To reclaim this specificity, there is a need for assessment models and methods that are sensitive to our disciplinary legacy.*
>
> (Yep, 2010, p. vii)

In our research, instructors indicated that they were indeed under increasing pressure to develop assessment procedures for the intercultural classroom that matched other quantitative measures being taken across the university. Assessment, while required, does not have to be monolithic. Rather, critical assessment strategies can and should be applied to the assessment of the intercultural communication course. Assessment must not be universal; rather, it should be developed to match the learning outcomes of the course.

BACKGROUND

Critical intercultural communication pedagogies seem incompatible with assessment; particularly, the neoliberal form that most universities require for accreditation. Specifically, Kahl (2013) explains, "Critical educators tend to reject assessment in part because of its tie to objective, neoliberal ideology, preferring that course learning be subjective and as free from objective assessment as possible" (p. 2615). Moreover, mounting pressure to develop universal tools of assessment exists as a way to measure and market the classroom as a commodity. Despite the negative sentiments felt by many (critical) educators, Kahl argues that assessment is a "necessary part of education" and can be incorporated positively by critical communication pedagogues (p. 2610). While traditional modes of assessment demonstrate a "positivistic bias" (Kahl, 2017, p. 117), we can make them more useful and suitable for the communication classroom (Yep, 2010). We rely heavily on Kahl's (2013, 2014, 2018) development of critical assessment strategies as we re-orient academic assessment to match critical commitments of intercultural pedagogies and promote teaching/learning practices that are accountable to those commitments.

Kahl (2013) differentiates between traditional assessment and assessment that happens through a lens of critical communication pedagogy, explaining that traditional modes test objective truths and levels of memorization. Traditional assessment is based on objective truth, which can be memorized, regurgitated, and measured. The correlating objectives/outcomes focus on observable skills. Critical assessment creates room for evaluating a student's ability to deconstruct their participation in hegemonic systems. Critical objectives/outcomes ask students to unpack issues of marginalization, privilege, and disparity. Kahl (2014) adds that as an added benefit, "when students are exposed to difficult questions of marginalization through hegemony in society, they become more engaged learners who are concerned with social justice, and, thus, they also become more engaged citizens who want to intervene in society" (pp. 38–39). Traditional modes of assessment are steeped in neoliberal ideologies and are a direct affront to Freirian (1970) contentions that memory banking should be problematized. Kahl's thoughts on critical assessment are applicable to the intercultural classroom because as he describes, "Critical objectives ask students to examine and question issues of power, class, privilege, hegemony, marginalization, sex, gender, and economic status" (Kahl, 2018, p. 38).

APPLYING CRITICAL ASSESSMENT TO INTERCULTURAL COMMUNICATION

Kahl's (2013) development of assessment through a critical communication pedagogy lens has been applied primarily to the basic course (i.e., Public Speaking). Though the concepts he discusses (e.g., hegemony and praxis) are clearly central in the Intercultural Communication course as well, additional student learning outcomes emerge when developing assessment tools for this course. In the National Communication Association's primer for

"Assessing" Intercultural Pedagogies for Social Justice   103

communication assessment, four steps for assessing the communication classroom are listed:

(1) Create clear objectives
(2) Focus on communication knowledge, skills, and attitudes
(3) Create an effective assessment plan
(4) Close the loop. (Backlund, Detwiler, Arneson, & Danielson, 2010, p. 17)

With these in mind, we offer some specificity for Intercultural Communication instructors.

Student Learning Objectives for the Intercultural Communication Course

Most institutions and accrediting bodies will require some form of "student learning outcomes" (SLOs) be present on syllabi and in course catalogues and learning management systems. These are the basis on which we assess what students are learning in each of our classes. These outcomes are best limited in number (lest we wish to spend all of our days assessing, rather than teaching), and should be worded in a way that the outcomes are "measurable." Before our critical readers run for the hills from such objective language, using Bloom's Taxonomy (1956) is one accessible way to word outcomes in ways that we can later assess (Figure 8.1).

Bloom's Taxonomy is a tool to help educators understand how learning can be achieved at the most basic and deeper levels. The foundation of learning,

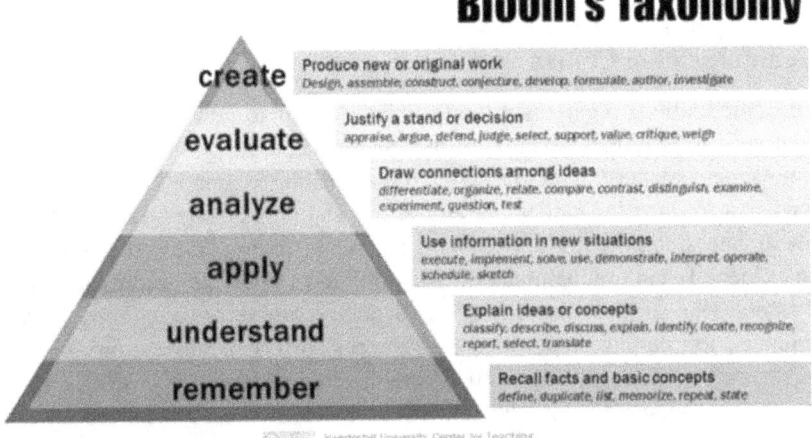

Figure 8.1. Bloom's Taxonomy.

as depicted in the model, is remembering information. The highest order of learning is at the apex of the pyramid—producing our own knowledge. Educators can keep such levels of learning in mind when developing courses at different levels (e.g., an introductory course may have more outcomes related to remembering and understanding, whereas an upper division or capstone course might focus on analysis and evaluation). Moreover, the words used to describe the type of learning that occurs at each level are *action* oriented and signal that a student is *doing* something that we can observe and assess.

Intercultural Communication, often an upper-division class, requires analysis, at the very least, and offers the possibility for students to evaluate and create. We believe that students in an Intercultural Communication course should achieve a basic understanding of the core concepts we have laid out in the previous chapters. Additionally, students should be able to practice critical reflexivity, empathy, ethnorelativism, and praxis. The following table offers examples of sample SLOs and forms of assessment (how we determine which outcome has been met) that might incorporate these concepts (see table 8.1). Many of the forms of assessment are described as "pedagogical activities" throughout the book and are included in the appendix.

When formulating student learning outcomes for intercultural communication, instructors can consider the following steps:

(1) Decide which level(s) of learning you would like students to achieve.
(2) Choose action-oriented words to phrase your SLOs.
(3) Create concrete, achievable goals for the course.
(4) Link SLOs to forms of assessment (e.g., this outcome will be assessed through student reflection papers).

Creating an Assessment Plan for the Intercultural Communication Course

For accreditation, most institutions will ask you to link Student Learning Outcomes to activities, exams, or assignments that will assess the students' achievement of these outcomes. As Howard (2003) reminds us in his reflections on a *Culturally Relevant Pedagogy*, we should be using a variety of ways to evaluate student learning. Howard urges us to ask, "Do I rely solely on paper, pencil, and oral responses? How often do I allow nontraditional means of assessment, such as role-playing, skits, poetry, rap, self-evaluations, Socratic seminars, journaling, student-led conferences, or cooperative group projects to be part of my class?" (p. 200). There are various ways to critically assess students' understanding in the intercultural communication classroom. The following are a few examples, but keep in mind that many of the activities we have included throughout the book can also be used to assess understanding.

Table 8.1. Sample Student Learning Outcomes and Corresponding Forms of Assessment for Intercultural Communication

Level of Knowledge	Possible SLOs	Form of Assessment
Remember	• By the end of this course, students should be able to define the central concepts and important influences in the field of intercultural communication. • By the end of this course, students should be able to describe the timeline of the emergence of intercultural communication as a field.	• Open-ended exam questions • Students draw timelines that include major turning points in the field (e.g., Foreign Service Institute, critical turn)
Understand	• By the end of this course, students should be able to discuss how one's culture shapes communication strategies • By the end of this course, students should be able to practice reflexivity about their own subjectivities in intercultural relationships.	• Students draft Wikipedia entries explaining major intercultural communication theories • Reflection journals
Apply	• By the end of this course, students should be able to apply and connect intercultural theories to everyday lived experiences. • By the end of this course, students should be able to apply theory to the experiences of others to better understand how the culture of others shapes your communication strategies.	• Intercultural alliances reflection paper • Prompts that reflect on intercultural experiences, using theories from the course • Intercultural transitions paper • Community-engaged Project
Analyze	• By the end of this course, students should be able to examine how social systems influence intercultural identities and relationships. • By the end of this course, students should be able to compare and contrast various models of identity development.	• Conflict analysis using Sorrells's multidimensional framework tool • Identity development reflection paper
Evaluate	• By the end of this course, students should be able to critique social policies that reproduce social inequalities and status-based hierarchies. • By the end of this course, students should be able to evaluate the pervasiveness of globalization. • By the end of this course, students should be able to critique geopolitical influences on culture.	• Supreme court dissent reflection paper • International conflict analysis paper
Create	• By the end of this course, students should be able to develop effective intercultural alliances. • By the end of this course, students should be able to investigate positions of power in everyday relationships.	• Intercultural alliances paper • Reflection journals • Community engaged project

Reflection Papers These three- to four-page papers that assess the understanding of concepts and theories.

This form of assessment asks students to *define* then *apply* concepts through an instructor-developed prompt. For example, the "Intercultural Alliances" reflection paper (Appendix K) included in this book asks students to articulate the major components of an intercultural alliance, citing where necessary, and apply these tenets to a relationship they have encountered. There are several examples of reflection papers throughout the book and in the appendix.

Community-Engaged Projects Sometimes referred to as *service-learning projects*, community-engaged learning asks students to work *with* local community members to address social issues while applying course concepts to what they observe. The Intercultural Communication course presents a unique opportunity for students to work with organizations that serve refugees, LGBTQ youth, or local cultural groups, for example. Such projects work best in conjunction with journaling, reflection papers, or group presentations to highlight and underscore the reciprocal and interdependent components of service and learning.

Free-Write Journals Similar to Kahl's (2013) assertion that autoethnographic writing helps students to identify avenues for praxis, free-write journals are a tool that help students to think about their own positionality and work toward critical reflexivity. Though these journals are named "free-write," they work best with prompts (see discussion questions embedded within each chapter). Free-writing several times throughout the semester, with a mid-way check-in, can help students begin to apply course concepts to their own lived realities. It is also a low-stakes tool for checking for basic understanding as instructors move toward higher-order levels of knowledge (e.g., analysis and evaluation).

Open-Ended Exams Open-ended exam questions work better than multiple-choice questions to assess students' ability to apply and evaluate information (Kahl, 2013). Asking students to "give an example" of the minority identity development model or "describe how" their avowed and ascribed identities differ offers a better assessment of how students move beyond the neoliberal principles of memory banking and toward conscientization. Utilizing the "discussion questions" we have listed at the end of each chapter may be a useful starting point for these questions.

Closing the Loop: Reflexivity and Intercultural Communication Assessment

There is no reason to collect assessment data if we do not plan to use the data to improve education for our students (Backlund et al., 2010). Intercultural Communication educators must create a process for analyzing assessment data and implementing changes based on the findings. In this sense, assessment is an ongoing process in which we continually review our goals for the class, update information, (re)educate ourselves about current trends, and think through the best forms of assessment as they link to the objectives we have so carefully crafted. Culture is fluid and ever evolving. The instruction of intercultural communication should follow suit. At the end of each cycle of assessment, we can ask ourselves the following questions to assess and adjust:

(1) To what extent did students learn what I thought they would?
(2) Are the objectives I crafted clear? What changes should be made?
(3) Are the objectives I crafted sufficiently couched within the current geopolitical climate?
(4) To what extent does my course include voices/readings from a variety of standpoints?
(5) How has my positionality (i.e., race, gender, sexuality, age, nationality, social class, religion, ability) influenced the content and objectives of this course?
(6) To what extent have I included students in discussion of their assessment?
(7) How can I continue to do what works well?

After reflecting on these questions, instructors can make a yearly plan for how they will improve their courses and subsequent assessment plan.

ADDITIONAL RESOURCES

National Communication Association Assessment Primer

This resource includes templates for building a departmental mission, program learning outcomes, curriculum maps, and rubrics. Rather than reinvent the wheel, the previously mentioned intercultural communication SLOs can be incorporated into a variety of these templates, which are often expected from accrediting bodies. It is worth noting, however, the focus of the National Communication Association (NCA) is on public speaking courses and objective forms of assessment.

KEY CHALLENGES

An obvious challenge of assessment in the course is adhering to college/university guidelines for assessment while implementing a critical vision of assessment. Some universities, for example, require a universal tool to be used for all departmental assessment, forcing instructors of Intercultural

Communication to subscribe to objective or "traditional" modes of assessment. Our advice is twofold: (1) supplement any required forms of objective assessment with critical assessment and (2) serve on committees that are responsible for developing assessment requirements, in hopes of offering a critical lens. Critically engaged faculty must be at the forefront of developing the assessment tools they are required to use "to help avoid the narrow focus on outcomes over which colleges have only limited control" and to keep the focus on learning (Roksa, Arum, & Cook, 2016, p. 7).

Related to institutional guidelines for assessment of learning is the end-of-the-semester student evaluations (a.k.a. teaching evolutions or student teaching evaluations) that has often become an institutionalized form of "assessing" teaching despite critiques that students might be rating personality (e.g., being enthusiastic) more than teaching effectiveness. Still, many institutions (over) rely on the student evaluations as one key mechanism for making decisions about whether or not to reappoint, tenure, or promote instructors. Responding to concerns of how gender-, race-, and sexuality-based stereotypes can negatively affect students' evaluations for women and minoritized faculty members, Lazos (2012) recommends that (a) institutions conduct "microanalysis of bias in student evaluations" based on gender, race, and sexual orientation; and (b) institutions "should think about teaching and the evaluative process more creatively" such as utilizing focus groups (p. 185). Similarly, to navigate politics around student teaching evaluations, we recommend implementing and recording your own student evaluations that are aligned with your learning objectives (e.g., mid-term evaluations); familiarize yourself with the role the student evaluations play in your institution; speak and strategize with your mentor(s) early on when challenges arise; and actively participate in conversations or serve on committees that make decisions about student evaluations if you have serious concerns and can afford the time.

Perhaps one of the biggest struggles for critically oriented instructors of Intercultural Communication is the lack of measurability for some course concepts. Put differently, not everything in the course can be made into a variable. Empathy, for example, is an affective process that cannot inherently be measured. Kahl (2013) explains, in these instances we must match the format of assessment to the format of learning. For example, if we engage students in a dialogue about empathy, we should offer them dialogic opportunities to demonstrate their knowledge about this subject through oral assessments or open-ended questions. Reflective assignments are our best option for capturing students' sensing and feelings around affective course concepts.

Finally, closing the loop on assessment is challenging because it requires instructors to be reflexive about their own teaching and how they might improve the quality of instruction. This is to say, if students are not meeting the outcomes that we, as instructors, prescribe then we must evaluate the modes of teaching and/or forms of assessment. This requires the instructor to take on the same tasks of examining power, privilege, hegemony, and identity in their quest to develop a strong and engaging intercultural communication pedagogy. To do so, we recommend keeping a teaching journal and making it a weekly or bi-weekly habit of jotting down and noting meaningful or memorable occurrences inside and outside the classroom.

STORIES FROM THE FIELD

John Oetzel, University of Waikato

As I write this entry, there are mass protests around the world about police brutality, white privilege, and systemic racism in response the horrific killing of George Floyd by police officer Derek Chauvin with his colleagues not intervening. I have read/watched news reports and followed social media posts about reactions to this act, protests, and various symbols (e.g., kneeling during the national anthem). I'm astonished at how hard it is for some (usually white) people to understand and accept systematic racism and white privilege. I also agreed with many who call of the need for true dialogue and listening to learn about these issues in order to create change. I think teachers of intercultural communication are well suited and have a responsibility to hold these dialogues and develop assessments in our classes that challenge students to learn about and reflect on these issues.

Developing assessments that help students understand systemic racism and white privilege and seek to change attitudes and behaviors is a challenge. When questioned or challenged about their views, people can become entrenched in their position and refuse to change. They may also shut down and not share their views. My goal as a teacher is to develop assessments that help students feel safe and also challenge them to enhance their knowledge, attitudes, and skills around intercultural communication. I accept that change is likely to be incremental for many.

I have developed two types of assessments that I think are useful to meet my goal: reflections about intercultural encounters and multi-level investigations about social and health inequities. For the first one, I ask students to identify positive and negative experiences of intercultural communication (either personal or something they witness or heard from someone close to them). I ask students to research what happened and why. Students have to use peer-reviewed research to explain the potential determinants of the episode (at societal/systemic and personal levels) and reflect on the experience including what they (or others) could do differently. I often use these experiences with permission in class discussions to illustrate the type of engagement

I am looking for. I find that students are able to have deep personal reflection and challenge their biases through this assessment.

The second assignment I often do in a group assignment. I ask students to think about the multi-level determinants of social and health inequities following a socio-ecological model. Inequities are well known and yet some students do not understand the wider determinants; they rely on individual decisions as the default. The students have to engage with the research literature at macro- (e.g., worldviews, media, systemic), meso- (e.g., communities, religious and work institutions), and micro- (e.g., family situation and individual behaviors) levels. I ask them to consider either which of these determinants are communication-based and/or how determinants affect intercultural communication. They then have to propose changes for enhancing intercultural communication. I find that this type of research and problem-solving results in personal engagement and change in attitudes.

Dr. Oetzel's assignments demonstrate how reflection assignments can help instructors to determine what students are learning, how they process information, and whether there is a transformation in attitudes toward intercultural identities and relationships. Activities like these are both engaging for the student and useful for intercultural instructors who are asked to assess transformative thinking and measure outcomes.

PEDAGOGICAL ACTIVITIES

Questions to the Author

Students can assess their own understanding of the course material by participating in a conversation with the author(s) of readings for class (embedded in Appendix G). In some cases, authors may be guest speakers and in others, the questions can be hypothetical. Students are asked to summarize the reading material for each course and pose questions that engage the material in direct relation to the course concepts and/or learning outcomes. While this assignment helps to assess student learning, it also increases student participation and engagement.

Reading Responses

Rather than (or in addition to) assessing learning through exams, reading responses offer students the opportunity to formulate their understandings and reactions to a reading prior to coming to class. In this assignment (embedded in Appendix H) students are asked to summarize the reading, discuss what they learned from the reading, explain larger social implications, and connect the current reading to those done previously in the course.

Conclusions and Reflections
Teaching Social Justice in a Changing and Challenging Moment

To critically love across our identity differences in the scholarly sense entails bearing witness to struggle, reaching out to nurture, marking the presence of privilege, and advocating for humanization. Critical love requires diving into the deep end of identity politics in our society which has created a firm hierarchy of whose pain is more worthy of public address.

(Griffin, 2012, p. 216)

Critical hope directly challenges inscribed habits of emotional inattention and signifies a willingness to exist within ambiguity and uncertainty. One knows, for example, that there is no assurance of justice, but one is yet willing to fight for justice.

(Boler, 2014, p. 36)

In this book, we have attempted to lay out and demonstrate what the classroom can look like when theories of (critical) intercultural communication and critical communication pedagogy intersect. The previous chapters should be seen as a demonstration of pedagogical praxis—applying theory to practice—in offering an overview of key concepts we have taught in the course, detailing the challenges of having these difficult conversations in the classroom, and exploring possible ways to navigate these challenges. In a way, teaching and learning intercultural communication for social justice becomes an embodied and reflexive practice of living by the theoretical commitments of critical intercultural communication pedagogy in everyday communication choices and interactions. Moreover, the activities we provide highlight the wealth of knowledge our field has to offer for new and continuing instructors. In total, we hope to have demonstrated pedagogical approaches for working toward social justice.

Teaching social-justice-based classes for social justice is intellectually complex, mentally draining, and emotionally charged, and thus requires more emotional labor than other classes we might teach (Lawless & Chen, 2019). But we get out so much more in many ways. Most books about teaching won't include a discussion on emotional labor, self-care, and mentoring because other courses don't require the strength and tenacity that Intercultural Communication demands. This course has its unique challenges and it is not for everybody. But if you choose to take on the task of teaching this course, it should be done with great care, heightened self-awareness, and critical reflection.

As I end my sabbatical, I feel rested and rejuvenated. I am ready to re-enter the Intercultural Communication classroom. This course has taken a lot from me over the years. I have cried. I have seethed. I have been left speechless. Still, I know that in the current political moment I have a responsibility to future generations to take what I have learned from my instructor-peers, intercultural experts, and a decade of teaching this course and spur discussions that can be transformative and thought-provoking. It can be difficult to take care of myself when attending to the varying intersectional needs of the students who take this course. This is a skill set that comes with trial and error, interparadigmatic discussion, and time. I used to say that I needed a "repertoire of responses" in order to respond to the seemingly innocuous, yet sometimes appalling things that students would say in this class. Though I have added to that repertoire, there are always new challenges that arise causing me to rethink my approach and communication. It is in this vein that I sought to share what I have found challenging and what I have learned along my pedagogical journey.

   I am re-committed to the process of teaching intercultural communication. That is to say that I am always learning about identities, contexts, histories, and experiences that are not my own. The best way to teach is to be open to learning. When I started teaching this course, I had no idea that I would, at some point, have to heed a warning that outside organizations like Turning Point USA and Campus Reform might plant students in my classes to record what I say and take things out of context. Alas, I have received such a warning and had to reaffirm my commitment to justice and rethink the way I would engage with new types of students. The cultural and political landscape of the United States is constantly changing. This means that new challenges will arise and I don't have all the answers. What we offer here is a start, to make the road a little less bumpy.

Looking back on my journey of teaching Intercultural Communication since fall 2008 across three universities through two terms of the Obama presidency and then the Trump administration, I most appreciate learning with and from students, especially how my students over time have pushed and challenged me to stay accountable and relevant as an intercultural communication scholar. At the same time, it has been a long and winding journey and now I feel more exhausted than excited. In the past twelve years, my approaches to this course as an immigrant woman and then mother-scholar of color have evolved not just in response to student populations in New Mexico, Ohio, and California but also adapting to changing institutional contexts (e.g., predominant white university vs. minority-serving institution) and political climates from Obama to Trump. The longer I am teaching this course, the more convinced I am that Intercultural Communication must be grounded in social justice even as it takes different forms. Also, if I were to speak with my younger self (a novice instructor teaching Intercultural Communication), I would remind her to be patient with herself and her students and lean as comfortably as possible on learning from mistakes because they are inevitable.

One of the driving forces for writing this book is the need that I see to advocate for what this course can be while pushing back on all the institutional and administrative constraints increasingly placed on a course like this. In 2016, I left my first tenure-track position in Ohio to join San Diego State University partly because I wanted the certainty of teaching Intercultural Communication every year so that I could better plan and prepare for it. Also, I longed to work with students from more diverse backgrounds, students who might share my lived struggles, and/or students who might see themselves reflected in me as the instructor standing in the front of the classroom. However, what I did not anticipate were the constraints that I have experienced having that certainty: losing out on a sabbatical had I stayed in Ohio, increased class sizes, fewer and fewer instructional resources, and higher expectation of what this course might accomplish in response to widening social gaps and inequities (e.g., #BlackLivesMatter, #MeToo, #IAmMuslim, and more). I am not someone who believes in fast work that is not informed by thoughtful deliberation and careful planning. I hope that this book gets across the deep commitment, resource, and investment necessary that makes possible teaching Intercultural Communication for social justice.

"CULTURAL" BATTLE FATIGUE AND SUSTAINABILITY

We would be disingenuous, even misleading, to discuss teaching (for) social justice without being honest about feeling vulnerable, if not wounded, and experiencing "cultural" battle fatigue in the process, especially when constantly speaking and teaching from intersecting identity positions of Otherness and marginalization. To illustrate, writing performatively as a queer feminist of color, Calafell (2010, 2015) narrates constructions of women of color as monstrous werewolf women in the academy. She explains, "I have been made to feel like a monster. I have been animalized, exoticized, tokenized, and sexualized. The 'excesses' of my body and my emotional affect mark me as a monstrous Other in the sanitized world of the white academy" (Calafell, 2015, p. 9). As an act of resistance, Calafell offers her vulnerable self in order to disrupt marginalization. As an immigrant woman of color, there definitely have been many times when I (Yea-Wen) enter spaces at my university feeling like going into the battleground or combat field (e.g., faculty meetings, trainings on implicit bias and microaggressions, and some class sessions). It would be unpopular to treat the classroom as a battleground or combat field given the interpersonal relationships between instructors and their students. However, if teaching for social justice aims to facilitate a cultural shift at individual, group, and institutional levels, at what point do instructors need to stand our grounds when encountering dismissive, demeaning, insensitive, and/or hostile interactions and/or bearing witness to such interactions between students? How might it be useful to theorize the classroom as a battleground for social justice? How might experiences of cultural battle fatigue serve some functions in the fight for social justice? In doing so, how could instructors and students attend to moments of injuries and address wounds in the process? If the college classroom such as the intercultural communication class is truly a key battleground for social justice in society, teachers and educators should not be fighting alone. How could we strategize together while sustaining ourselves and supporting one another within U.S. universities that prefer and promote individualism and competition often in the name of "excellence"?

On the basis of the experiences of Black and African Americans, Smith (2004) conceptualizes racial battle fatigue as "a response to the distressing mental/emotional conditions that result from facing racism daily," including contentious classrooms (p. 180). Expanding Smith's concept of racial battle fatigue, we consider "cultural battle fatigue" that social-justice educators and warriors experience on a daily basis in response to distressing conditions. Cultural battle fatigue in teaching intercultural communication for social justice can manifest in various ways. The following are what we ourselves have experienced. First, the process of creating the classroom space for minoritized, marginalized, and historically silenced voices to speak (and hopefully be heard) can make the instructor vulnerable to challenges, if not resistance, from students, especially racially unaware whites, males, and heterosexuals occupying privileged and dominant group positions. Boler (2014) terms such resistance as manifestation of "suffering from 'dominant cultural withdrawal'" (p. 27). Further, she argues that, when instructors develop or show compassion toward all students' suffering, compassion facilitates change as she states "I must be able to meet their discomfort with compassion—and with resources to help them replace the lost sense of self" (Boler, 2014, p. 37). Second, centering marginality in the classroom also means ensuring that such voices are heard on their own terms, which requires the instructors to be proactive about and mindful of how to show compassion and care for students when they become triggered, wounded, or reinjured in the process. Third, instructors teaching intercultural communication are often expected to lead and facilitate difficult conversations well and still receive high teaching evaluations at the end of the semester. When problems occur or students complain or push back, the instructors often feel like they are supposed to deal with the consequences alone. Fourth, on top of being women, immigrants, and/or people of color, many instructors of intercultural communication might be the only one or one of the few in the department who talk about diversities and teach communication with critical commitments to social justice, which is a heavy layer of burden on its own. Ashby-King and Hanasono (2019) state, "Communication discipline does its students a disservice by only discussing diversity in intercultural communication courses" (p. 2). Each moment of fatigue might be like a papercut, a mosquito bite, or a minor burn. Cumulatively, moments of cultural battle fatigue can add up, and, when untreated, a minor burn gets worse, more damaging, and even harmful over time. If we agree that the feeling of cultural battle fatigue is inevitable, let's push for communal, institutional, and disciplinary support to properly attend to such cuts or wounds so that we all can keep fighting the good fight.

EMOTIONAL LABOR AND SELF-CARE

The labor of teaching and learning Intercultural Communication is not just intellectual work but also equally emotional work. Our interviews with Intercultural Communication instructors demonstrate that almost all participants experienced some form of emotional labor in their work related to this course in particular (Lawless & Chen, 2019). The unwritten expectation that professors, especially women, people of color, and minoritized group members perform emotional tasks such as challenging racism, responding to attacks, caretaking of vulnerable students, and creating space for vulnerability around sensitive topics is especially apparent in the Intercultural Communication classroom. That is to say that these instructors did not feel the same amount of emotion with work when speaking about other courses such as Public Speaking. In conversations with instructors teaching this course we learned it is not uncommon to feel empty, exhausted, and drained at the end of a class session, let alone an entire semester. Multiple instructors said that this course had brought them to tears. One individual reflected that they mentored a young instructor who was new to teaching the course who said she would "never teach the course again" after the emotional rollercoaster she experienced when teaching it.

Taking emotional labor out of the course is not possible because of the political topics and social issues that inevitably come up, especially when teaching from a critical perspective. Emotional labor sheds lights on not just the study of Intercultural Communication as a political project, but also institutional and disciplinary politics surrounding the intricate yet often unspoken relationship between a course like Intercultural Communication or a course in Ethnic Studies and the university's struggle with—if not reluctance to—serve its minoritized students. However, there are ways to care for oneself when continuing to teach the course semester after semester. Self-care is all-too-important in balancing emotional labor. Thus, we recommend, in addition to planning lessons and activities for the course, dedicating some time to strategize self-care and support if not survival strategies for navigating emotional labor. Here are some examples:

Figure 9.1. 9 × 9 Healthy Tips.

These ideas and others help to center your own needs in your ongoing work to learn and teach about connecting with others. Making space for your physical and mental well-being will help you to create a sustainable path for continuing this important work in the Intercultural Communication classroom.

MENTORING

It's been our premise throughout this book that Intercultural Communication is one of the most offered courses in communication studies, yet it comes with little training compared to Public Speaking. Although basic pedagogical principles can be applied across multiple courses within and across the discipline, Intercultural Communication requires additional training and expertise. Ideally, graduate programs and colleges would offer the specific training needed to teach Intercultural Communication or other courses highlighting issues of difference and social justice. Given the slim chances of a massive overhaul of our discipline's minimum pedagogical standards, we advocate for an extensive mentorship program within and across colleges and universities. Some of the knowledge needed to teach this course comes from experience. It is our hope that those who have some or a great deal of experience would be willing to share it.

Considering the complexity of both what teaching Intercultural Communication for social justice entails and how a university functions in relation to this course, we advocate a broad approach to mentoring for this course. See Appendix N for a mentoring map for new intercultural instructors that is inspired by the work of National Center for Faculty Development and Diversity (NCFDD). What is important in this mentor map is the idea that one mentor is unable to meet all the divergent needs of a mentee. Also, mentoring really takes a village approach. Along this line of thinking, we would advocate a village approach to mentoring for this course.

ADVOCATING FOR THE PRESENT AND THE FUTURE OF THE FIELD

Intercultural Communication, though a field in its early stages, has much to offer broader teaching and learning about communicating and relating across difference in an increasingly diversified and globalized world. The topics we have covered here—philosophical assumptions, identities, power/privilege, alliances, ideologies, globalization, community engagement, and assessment—do not occur in a vacuum. These topics are at the heart of broader discussions of diversity and inclusion, equity and social justice, and human rights. We see instructors of Intercultural Communication positioned at the forefront of the discussions that are at the heart of many university missions and more than ever, in public discourse.

At the time of writing this book, the resurgence of national movements like Black Lives Matter highlight the necessity for understanding the topics we have outlined in these pages. It is easy to see polarized political views when watching the news and reading a social media feed. It is more difficult to use the tools necessary to analyze the underlying *ideologies* of white supremacy and meritocracy as they relate to the lived realities of Black and Brown bodies/*identities*. Calls for white *allies* to show up and use their voice to amplify those of Black activists have taken over social media. We can see *global-local* connections as we witness an uprising that has spread across the globe, spurring the largest international protest in modern history. More individual conversations about *privilege and power* as they relate to individuals *and* systems occur as we see leaders of the movement ask for "defunding the police." In this one social moment, we can engage several of the concepts at the heart of intercultural communication. Imagine the impact that this field can have as we engage these topics with thousands of students over time. Intercultural Communication provides the tools and language for ongoing analysis of communication on an individual level, within relationships, and as connected to larger social discourse. Instructors of these topics have much opportunity and responsibility in leading this charge.

It is also our responsibility to promote these values outside of the classroom walls. Universities, operating under a neoliberal framework, are pushing to offer diversity certificates and create a singular "diversity requirement" for all students. While it is important to learn about diversity, these efforts often end up commodifying intercultural communication as a singular skill that students can collect for their toolkit, rather than a way of thinking and living that transforms understandings and personal commitments. We hope that this book both helps instructors to navigate the challenges in the classroom and promotes the assumption that Intercultural Communication is about making the world a more just and connected place by attending to oppressions and inequalities rooted in cultural differences. We write this book because we believe and feel in our hearts that critical intercultural communication pedagogy, with its promises and limitations, holds generative potentials in simultaneously resisting forces that undervalue and undermine education and reimagining learning spaces that can propel positive changes to make a difference in the world. We see this book as one of the beginnings of more organized and systematic efforts to develop and practice critical intercultural communication pedagogy in an increasingly globalized and uncertain world. Join us in this commitment to working with students for social justice and communicating an ethic of critical love and hope.

CRITICAL INTERCULTURAL COMMUNICATION ACTIVITIES

Appendix A

Creating a Community: Working through the First Day/Week of Class

Creating a space that accepts discomfort, promotes an anti-racist agenda, and encourages dialogue starts on the first day of class. In the following, we detail several considerations for the first week that will help to improve the connectedness/openness of the community for the rest of the semester.

LAND ACKNOWLEDGMENT

In your syllabus or during your first meeting, consider reading a land acknowledgment. Land acknowledgments exist to mark the ongoing process of colonialism in the spaces we live, work, and learn. The Native Governance Center has several tools to help build your own land acknowledgments (see https://nativegov.org/a-guide-to-indigenous-land-acknowledgment/). Many universities and departments have written land acknowledgments. In online or remote learning environments, it can be helpful to ask students to research the land from which they live/work and place acknowledgments in the chat or discussion board. By doing this on the first day of class, instructors demonstrate reflection, analysis, and praxis—tools that should be fostered throughout the course.

COMMUNITY AGREEMENTS

Building a set of community agreements is a collaborative process that creates expectations for how communication should unfold in the classroom. Agreements are developed together with students and instructors and aim to create a space in which the course concepts can be discussed respectfully as the class works toward social justice. The instructor may have some important contributions that work toward anti-racism and equity, rather than the common proclamation that "all opinions should be valued equally." Instead, this should be an exercise in which you encourage students to lean into discomfort and brainstorm ways of handling such feelings when they arise. Community agreements should be valuable for returning to if/when resistance or misunderstanding arises in class discussions. While the list should be generated by the community, some common things to include might be: (a) We will keep an open mind, (b) we will step up (if we don't often take up space) and step back (if we are taking up too much space), (c) we will listen before responding, and (d) we will treat others the way they want to be treated. You might consider if you want to have an overt anti-racist, anti-sexist, anti-ableist, anti-homophobic, and anti-transphobic agenda. Now would be the time to interject these guidelines.

ICEBREAKERS

Building community relies to some extent on a commitment to be vulnerable. One icebreaker that may help to emphasize this is to build a *community web*. In this activity, the instructor holds a ball of yarn and explains the following:

> *I would like us to build a strong community. Communities require a commitment to each other. I am going to hold onto one end of this yarn and tell you two things: One thing I have to offer to this community and one thing I would appreciate from the community. Then, I will throw the ball (while holding on to my end) to one other member of this community. That person should state their gift and desire, hold on to one part of the yarn, and throw the ball to someone else. The transition should continue until we are all holding on to the yarn and everyone has shared.*

The result is a web of interaction. When everyone has participated, you can ask the students to pull the yarn tight—this indicates a strong community in which you can see the connection and intention. When students let their yarn sag, it shows a week community without much commitment. Use the activity to create a space where students can share their fears, weaknesses, strengths, and desires. Return to those commitments throughout the semester.

RESOURCES

Because the content of the course can be emotional particularly for Black, Indigenous, and other people of color and other marginalized groups, it is important to provide resources for students who wish to learn more or have additional discussions about course materials and experiences. For example, find out if your college/university has an Intercultural Center or other student resources on campus related to identities (e.g., LGBTQ Resource Center, Women's Center, Black Student Union).

Appendix B

Privilege and Disadvantage Inventory

Adapted from appendix 3M in *Teaching for Diversity and Social Justice*, Second Edition, Routledge, 2007.

Objective: Create a space for participants to reflect on their experiences with both privilege and disadvantage

Materials needed:

- Copies of the privilege and disadvantage inventory for all participants.

Instructions:

- Ask participants to read and respond to all statements on the inventory. Circle the T if the statement is true for them. Circle the F if the statement is not.

Sample inventory statements:

- T or F: Most of the adults and other students in the high school I attended had a racial or ethnic heritage similar to mine.
- T or F: I was raised in a single-parent household.
- T of F: My family has taken vacations outside of the United States.

Debriefing questions:

- What are your reactions to completing this exercise?
- If any, what statements were particularly striking to you, and why?
- How might this exercise raise questions about power, privilege, and disadvantage for you?

Appendix C

The Beads of Privilege

Adapted from https://feministagendapdx.files.wordpress.com/2012/06/beadsofprivilege.pdf.

Objective: Create a space for participants to experience and process how privilege functions intersectionally in society.

Materials needed:

- Strings or bands to make bracelets
- As many different-colored beads to represent different social/cultural categories and groups
- Tape to hang up questions
- Dishes for people to put their beads in while they walk around
- Dishes to hold the beads.

Descriptions:

- Set up dishes with beads representing different social/cultural groups around the room.
- Each dish of beads is accompanied by a question sheet with specific ways in which privilege works for those belonging to the particular group. For example, blue beads could symbolize religious privilege. Students would take a bead for every religion-based statement that applies to them.
- Instruct students to walk around the room in silence, read the question sheets, and gather beads. Students can make their bracelets or key chains with the beads.
- Debrief the activity.

Sample privilege statements for different question sheets:

- Race privilege:

    "I can turn on the television or open to the front page of the paper and see people of my race widely represented."

- Christian privilege:

    "My place of work or school is closed on your major religious holidays."

- Gender privilege: "I do not worry about walking alone at night."

Appendix D

Privilege Walk/Exercise

Adapted from "Privilege Exercise" by 1994/2005 National Curriculum & Training Institute, Inc.

Objective: Assist participants to see/feel how people may face inequities in daily interactions.

Materials needed:

- Generate a list of activity statements for conducting the exercise.
- Need a large enough space so that participants can comfortably line up in a straight line.

Instruction:

- Politely request that participants line up in a straight line across the activity area.
- Explain to the participants that you will read a list of statements. The participants are to listen carefully and follow the direction at the end of each statement.
- Read through all activity statements.
- After having read all statements, have participants remain in their final positions and look at their own position in relation to other participants' positions in the room. Pause for a moment for noting.
- Have participants pair up and share their personal thoughts and feelings about their final positioning.
- Process as a group.

Sample activity statements:

- If your ancestors were forced to come to the United States, take one step back.
- If you were ever called names because of your race, class, ethnicity, gender, religion, nationality, or sexual orientation, take one step back.

- If you were raised in an area where there was prostitution, drug activity, and so on, take one step back.
- If you studied the culture of your ancestors in elementary school, take one step forward.
- If there were more than fifty books in your house when you grew up, take one step back.

Debriefing questions:

- Was this exercise comfortable for you? Why or why not?
- Did any of the questions cause anyone to feel devalued in any way? Why or why not?
- To what extent do you find this exercise useful and to what aim?
- What observations have you made about this activity?
- How did your environment influence your response to this activity?
- In your experience, what considerations are necessary when interacting with persons who were socialized with or exposed to a different set of rules or ideas than you?

Recommendations:

- This exercise is considered high risk. We would recommend this exercise only if it is with a relatively small group of students who already know one another on a personal level. Also, debriefing is absolutely key.
- Ultimately, this exercise aims for a shift in perspective about one's self in relation to others. If folks are not comfortable with one another, doing so might create more defensiveness than allowing learning that can result in a shift in perspective.

Appendix E

Cultural Identity Pyramid

In the following space, reflect on how you have experienced your cultural identities in interactions with others (e.g., ability, socioeconomic status, nationality, sex and gender, age, sexual orientation, spirituality, race, ethnicity, and regionality). What cultural identities, if any, do you think about all the time? What cultural identities are easy for you to talk about with others, and what cultural identities are difficult, and why? Are there cultural identities of yours that you rarely think about, and why might that be? Specifically, organize your cultural identities into three types as shown in the cultural identity pyramid in the following text. At the bottom of the pyramid, list your **core identity(ies)** that shape or constitute who you are as a person. In the middle of the pyramid, list your **salient identity(ies)** that you are often aware of in everyday situations across a number of contexts. At the top of the pyramid, list your **contextual identity(ies)** that you think about only in a certain context or with certain people.

Appendix E

Identity Triangle Hierarchy.

Appendix F

Avowed and Ascribed Identity Charts

Instruction: Draw *two* identity pie charts that describe your multiple identities. Consider your "selves" that are important or meaningful to you and focus on groups that you are a member of or belong to. One identity pie chart represents how you view your selves. In this pie chart, draw your self-avowed identities (i.e., how *you* view yourself): "*I am* _____." The other identity pie chart represents how you think others view you. Draw your other-labeled identities: "*You are* _____."

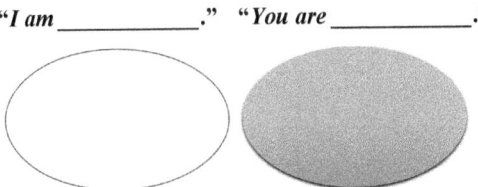

"*I am* _____."   "*You are* _____."

Empty Oval and Shaded Oval.

After you have finished your two identity pie charts, find a classmate whom you have not interacted with and introduce yourself using the two identity pie charts. It is okay to share only to the extent that you are comfortable. Please note both similarities and differences.

Pair Discussion Questions:

1. How would you compare and contrast your two identity pie charts?
2. What does this activity illustrate about the nature of "identity"?

Appendix G

Intercultural Communication
　Sample Syllabus 1
　(A service-learning course, using a textbook)

Instructor name:
Office hours:
Instructor contact info:
Meeting day(s) and time:
Meeting location:
Number of units:

Course description: In a sense, Intercultural Communication is about unpacking, challenging, and problematizing the ways in which "we see the world as we are." This course offers a survey and critique of major theories, concepts, and issues in intercultural communication encounters. This course will be conducted as a seminar with the goal of engaging with and interrogating issues, theories, and practices in intercultural communication. Taking a critical and global perspective, we will consider, explore, and examine the ways in which culture and communication interact, intersect, and affect each other. In particular, we will consider how globalization impacts our cultural practices, intercultural relations, and cross-cultural interactions.

　What students can expect to learn in the course (course learning outcomes):

- experience direct intercultural encounters with Asian immigrants and/or Asian Americans through partnership with Asian Community Alliance, Inc.

- develop an appreciation of major issues, theories, and perspectives in intercultural communication scholarship.
- develop critical perspectives and increase awareness on global and local issues related to intercultural communication.
- Practice, via service learning, intercultural praxis and develop an ability to translate and transform theoretical understanding of intercultural communication into practices in everyday life.

REQUIRED TEXTS AND READINGS

Sorrells, S. (2013). *Intercultural communication: Globalization and social justice*. Thousand Oaks: SAGE.

*Additional readings are available through our course management system.

COURSE POLICIES

**Your university will likely include many required policies to be included in this section. In addition to these boiler plate policies, we recommend the two following sections:

Diversity, Equity, and Inclusion: This course encourages different perspectives related to such factors as race, sex and gender, ethnicity, sexuality, religion, nationality, abilities, socioeconomic standing, immigration status, and other relevant cultural identities. This course seeks to foster understanding and inclusiveness related to such diverse perspectives, ways of knowing, and ways of communicating. You will learn best by listening to those voices that have historically been silenced, making room for discomfort, and opening yourself up to change. I will foster an anti-racist classroom where we strive for equity and justice for all. This is reflected in our readings, discussions, and other classroom materials.

Participation and Engagement: We will engage the topics presented in this class as a community, with shared goals. This class is designed for active student participation, and engagement is a necessary, important, and required part of this course. Your engagement is what will bring meaning to the information in this class and make this class worthwhile for you and others. Engagement may look like (but is not limited to) any of the following:

- Attending class regularly and choosing to be present
- Completing the reading before class
- Participating in classroom discussions
- Participating in class activities

- Speaking your truth
- Listening actively
- Stepping up or stepping back when it comes to speaking in class
- Applying course concepts to life outside the course

Grading: Insert the scale and explanation for how grades will be determined.

ASSIGNMENTS

1. Participation

(a) Question to the Author

Length: 100+ words

When everyone reads the assigned material before coming to class, it helps us to have more thoughtful, engaging, and productive discussions in class. It also ensures that you are keeping up with the readings. To achieve that aim, you will submit one to two questions addressed to the author of the textbook on the assigned chapter. Your question(s) should function as a conversation starter, rather than simply soliciting information. You are expected to do the following:

1. Use the first two to three sentences summarizing a key idea or issue in the assigned chapter that pique your curiosity. Please cite the page number.
2. Use the next few sentences developing a question or two around the summary.
3. Post your questions on the appropriate discussion forums on Blackboard by Sunday midnight each week.

Each question should be at least 100 words and carefully reflect the content of the assigned chapter. Your question(s) should help us (a) generate new ideas, (b) evaluate/critique the ideas presented in the textbook, and/or (c) make connections between different issues/ideas. Don't be afraid to be a devil's advocate to facilitate new ways of thinking. I will select a few questions and incorporate them into our in-class discussions.

(b) In-Class Activities

You are expected to come to class abreast of the issues, ready to contribute and to help shape our shared understandings and frameworks. At various junctures, you will be asked to prepare written responses, examples, and reflections and participate in various activities in class.

2. Autobiography of Racialized Body

Length: 4–5 pages, *containing no more than two spelling, grammar, or punctuation errors per page* (no shorter than 3.5 pages and no longer than 5.5 pages)

Note: This assignment is adapted from McKinney (2008).
Everyone has some racial and/or ethnic heritage, which may be more visible and/or important for some and less so for others. In this paper, you will reflect on and write about your personal life story(ies), or autobiography, focusing on experiences that you have had with race and/or ethnicity. Since identities are multiple, overlapping, and intersecting, your experiences with race might relate to other relevant identities such as sex and gender, sexuality, class, and so on. The point of this assignment is not to reinforce racial/ethnic categories but to expose hidden, or unconscious, assumptions about race and/or ethnic groups that hinder productive intergroup interactions.

Throughout your paper, use as many specific, concrete, and detailed examples and write about as many experiences, memories, and stories as you can. Choose stories from your life when you were most aware of race and/or ethnicity. Use details to try to describe and process your thoughts and experiences as thoroughly as possible. This paper should read like a common autobiography but with a particular focus on issues of race and/or ethnicity. Reflect on things that have happened to you. First, tell a story about something that has happened to you, and then add something you learned from it. *This paper is about your personal experiences with race/ethnicity, not what you think about issues of race/ethnicity nor current racial issues.* Focus on occurrences like change, turning points, memorable moments, feelings, conflicts, and recurring themes.

Write about a specific instance that you remember as being significant to you with regard to your race and/or ethnicity. *What I am looking for is the budding awareness, shifts, progression, or other development of your racial/ethnic consciousness.* Be specific. It helps to work and write chronologically from the first time you remember becoming aware of your or someone else's race/ethnicity to the present. Following are some guiding questions to help you start:

- What are some of your first memories of becoming aware of racial/ethnic differences and your place in a racial/ethnic group?
- What messages did your family communicate to you about your own race/ethnicity as you were growing up?
- What messages did your family communicate to you about members of other racial/ethnic groups as you were growing up?

- Does/did your family have specific traditions related to your racial/ethnic heritage? How do you think this compares with other families or your same race/ethnicity? How about with other families of other races/ethnicities?
- How, if at all, have your ideas about race/ethnicity changed through the years?
- What specific world events, personal incidents, relationship with significant others, environmental factors, media images, and so on, have had an effect on your ideas about race, ethnicity, and racism?
- What are some experiences that have made your race/ethnicity most visible to you?
- Have you been subject to discrimination based on race/ethnicity? If so, what happened?
- How do you think demographic changes that are currently underway will affect your experiences and attitudes related to race, ethnicity, and racism?
- Do you think racism is becoming more of or less of a problem in the United States? If you think it is a problem, what do you think the best solution(s) is/are?

You will be graded on the depth of your reflections and on whether you follow the directions for the assignment. Be sure to (a) meet the page length and formatting requirements for the paper; (b) proofread your essay flawlessly; (c) focus on stories, instances, and experiences, not opinions; and (d) demonstrate careful thought in the context of things that we have been discussing in class.

3. Decoding Popular Culture Presentation

Due: The day you sign up for
Time: Fifteen minutes, three people in each group
Requirement: Outline, works cited, and PowerPoint or equivalent visual aid

This assignment asks you to conduct an analysis of a popular cultural text of your choice. Following the explanations in chapter 6 on Encoding and Decoding (pp. 135–138), you will decode, analyze, and come up with a *dominant*, *negotiated*, and *oppositional* reading of the chosen cultural text. Also, to aid your decoding, analysis, and interpretation, you are required to incorporate three to four concepts from the textbook and two outside academic sources. Include both in-text citations and references following *APA 6th Edition*.
   Suggested procedure:

1. Choose a cultural text. Your cultural text may include:
    - Movie
    - TV show (episode)

- TV commercial
- Music video
- Book
- Magazine advertisement
- Political campaign
- News articles

2. Develop your analysis using a dominant, negotiated, and oppositional reading.
   - Incorporate three to four key terms from the textbook.
   - Each group member should reflect on how your positionality and standpoint inform and shape the way you decode and interpret the text.
   - Your analysis should be original, unique, and thought-provoking.

3. Organize your analyses and academic sources into a summary report.
   - Use the essay format: Intro, main points, and conclusion.
   - Provide in-text citations and a list of references in APA style.

4. Put together a PowerPoint presentation (following Buzzfeed style if you are comfortable with this style). Here is an example: http://www.buzzfeed.com/henrygoldman/what-its-like-to-be-in-an-interracial-couple.

   - Introduction: Begin with an attention getter. Then, briefly explain the cultural text; state the reason why you chose the text; state your thesis statement and preview of main points.
   - Main points: Your slides should be organized according to major ideas of your analysis and findings. Use a clear organizational structure. Limit the amount of texts on each slide. Include the citations of any sources you use. Use texts and images effectively.
   - Conclusion: Briefly summarize the main points; discuss the significance of your findings; leave with a concluding remark.
   - A list of sources following *APA 6th Edition*.

The group will be graded on the organization of the summary report and presentation, content, depth of analysis, originality of interpretation, presentational aids, and the overall presentation.

4. Service-Learning Assignments

Service learning in this course refers to the process of structured experiential learning that internationally supports intercultural communication and community needs equally. Service learning is one of the most important components of this course. The purpose of this assignment is to provide you with opportunities to work with people from different cultural backgrounds;

cultivate your intercultural communication skills; and learn about the experiences of immigrants, refugees, and racial minorities in the United States.

(a) Service-Learning Journals

Length: Two to three pages per journal entry, containing no more than two spelling, grammar, or punctuation errors per page.

Throughout the course of working on the service learning project, you will submit a total of three journals reflecting on your experience by integrating your personal insights with the course content. The journaling will include but not limited to:

- reflecting on the process of completing the service learning project with a focus on your responsibilities at the experience (e.g., what was accomplished; what were your specific duties; any surprises that you encountered)
- describing and reflecting on your learning—or "metamorphosis" if applicable—over the time period of the experience (e.g., what knowledge did you gain about yourself; any difficulties or challenges experienced in completing the tasks you were assigned to do)
- reflecting on any connections and applications of intercultural communication concepts and content discussed in this class
- describing your insight, suggestions, or recommendations for the service learning project.

(b) Service-Learning Presentation

Requirement: Outline, works cited, and PowerPoint or equivalent visual aid

In partnership with Asian Community Alliance (ACA), each group will work on a twenty-hour service learning project that helps ACA to achieve its mission of serving Asian and Asian American communities in the great Cincinnati area. I will ask for ACA staff feedback on your participation and citizenship.

Put together a PowerPoint presentation to share with the class and ACA staff your service learning project. Your presentation will include but not limited to:

- Introduction: Begin with an attention getter. Then, briefly explain the nature of your project; state your thesis statement and preview of main points.
- Main points: Your slides should be organized according to major ideas of your analysis and findings. Use a clear organizational structure. Limit the amount of texts on each slide. Include the citations of any sources you use. Use texts and images effectively.

- Conclusion: Briefly summarize the main points; discuss the significance of your findings; leave with a concluding remark.
- A list of sources following APA 6th Edition.

The group will be graded on the organization of the summary report and presentation, content, depth of analysis, originality of interpretation, presentational aids, and the overall presentation.

5. Intercultural Praxis Paper

Length: six to eight pages, *containing no more than two spelling, grammar, or punctuation errors per page* (no shorter than 5.5 pages and no longer than 8.5 pages)
Recommendation: Keep a weekly intercultural communication journal.

The purpose of this assignment is to develop and enhance your intercultural communication skills through critical self-assessment and reflections. Throughout the semester, pay attention to your everyday interactions with other people. I recommend keeping a weekly journal for reflections, key activities, and thought-provoking events. You will write an eight- to ten-page paper describing, reflecting, and assessing your intercultural experience(s) and discuss what it means for you to exercise intercultural praxis (see chapter 1). Clearly describe specific incidents or interactions that illustrate (or not) your intercultural communication skills, and describe/assess your own intercultural communication strengths and continued needs. Be sure to include what you have learned throughout this semester and also include additional research findings. You are required to incorporate ***a minimum of three academic sources***. Your sources should consist of academic journal articles that review actual research on intercultural relationships, communication, and praxis. Internet sources such as web pages, unless used to access academic libraries, journals, and research, should not be used. *You are welcome to use the readings in this class for your paper, but they do not count toward the six required sources.* Use 12-size font, 1-inch margins, and double spacing. Also, cite sources both in text and in references utilizing *APA 6th Edition*. Proofread your paper before submitting. In essence, your paper should consist of three main parts: (a) describe and reflect on what kinds of intercultural communicator you are drawing from specific incidents or interactions (such as the field trip to Cincinnati); (b) assess your own intercultural communication strengths and continued needs; and (c) provide five to seven conclusions or key recommendations for applying intercultural praxis to everyday situations. *Incorporate relevant research findings in appropriate places.*

6. Exams

You will participate in two exams in this class in which you demonstrate your understanding of the course material. Each will consist of true/false, multiple-choice, matching, and/or fill-in-the-blank questions. You are responsible for *all* materials covered in the text as well as *all* materials covered in class, including supplemental readings and guest presentations.

Course schedule: Assigned readings and major writing (or other types of) assignments with due dates.

Table 1. Appendix 9—Example of Syllabus with Service Learning Component

Week	Date	Topic	Reading
1	M	Course Overview	
	W	Cultural Identity Inventory	
	F	Ch. 1 Opening the Conversation	Read Ch. 1
2	M	Ch. 1 continued	Read *Nakagawa (2016), "Praxis what you breach"
	W	Introducing to Service Learning Community Partner	
	F	Ch. 2 Understanding the Context of Globalization	Read Ch. 2
3	M	**Labor Day Holiday—No Classes**	
	W	Ch. 2 Understanding the Context of Globalization	
	F	Ch. 3 Globalizing Body Politics: Embodied Verbal and Nonverbal Communication	Read Ch. 3
4	M	Ch. 3 continued	
	W	Multiculturalism and Colorblindness	Read *Chen, Simmons, & Kang (2015), Multiracial/Multicultural Obama-ism
	F	Body Politics under the Obama Presidency	
5	M	Ch. 4 (Dis)Placing Culture and Cultural Space: Locations of Nonverbal and Verbal Communication	Read Ch. 4
	W	Ch. 4 continued	
	F	*Service-Learning Project Time # 1*	
6	M	Guest Speakers from Community Partner	
	W	Ch. 5 Crossing Borders: Migration and Intercultural Adaptation	Read Ch. 5
	F	Ch. 5 continued	
7	M	**Exam #1**	
	W	Ch. 6 Jamming Media and Popular Culture: Analyzing Messages about Diverse Culture	Read Ch. 6
	F	Ch. 6 continued	

Week	Date	Topic	Reading
8	M	Ch. 7 Privileging Relationships: Intercultural Comm. in Interpersonal Contexts	Read Ch. 7
	W	Ch. 7 continued	Read *Chen & Torigoe (2016), Discourses of Interracial Romantic Couples
	F	Workshop Day on Decoding Popular Culture Presentations	
9	M	**Decoding Popular Culture Presentations Part I**	
	W	**Decoding Popular Culture Presentations Part II**	
	F	**Decoding Popular Culture Presentations Part III**	
10	M	Ch. 8 The Culture of Capitalism and the Business of Intercultural Communication	Read Ch. 8
	W	Ch. 8 continued	
	F	*Service-Learning Project Time # 2*	
11	M	Ch. 9 Negotiating Intercultural Conflict and Social Justice: Strategies for Intercultural Relations	Read Ch. 9
	W	Ch. 9 continued	
	F	*Service-Learning Project Time # 3*	
12	M	Ch. 10 Engaging Intercultural Communication for Social Justice: Challenges and Possibilities for Global Citizenship	Read Ch. 10
	W	**Veterans Day Holiday—No Classes**	
	F	Ch. 10 Continued	
13	M	*Service-Learning Project Time # 4*	
	W	*Service-Learning Project Time # 5*	
	F	*Service-Learning Project Time # 6*	
14	M	Review and Workshop Day on Service-Learning Presentations	
	W	**Thanksgiving Break—No Classes**	
	F	**Thanksgiving Break—No Classes**	
15	M	**Service-Learning Presentations Part I**	
	W	**Service-Learning Presentations Part II**	
	F	Exam #2	

LIST OF ADDITIONAL READINGS

Chen, Y.-W., Simmons, N., Kang, D. (2015). "My family isn't racist—however . . .": Multiracial/Multicultural Obama-ism as an ideological barrier to teaching intercultural communication. *Journal of International and Intercultural Communication, 8*(2), 167–186. doi:10.1080/17513057.2015.1025331

Chen, Y.-W., & Torigoe, C. (2016). "We get bad looks, all the time": Ideologies and identities in the discourses of interracial romantic couples. In K. Sorrells & S. Sekimoto (Eds.), *Globalizing intercultural communication: A reader* (pp. 144–155). Thousand Oaks, CA: SAGE.

Nakagawa, G. (2016). "Praxis what you breach": Intercultural praxis, impersonation, and stereotyping. In K. Sorrells & S. Sekimoto (Eds.), *Globalizing intercultural communication: A reader* (pp. 13–21). Thousand Oaks, CA: SAGE.

Appendix H

> **Intercultural Communication**
> **Sample Syllabus 2**
> **(An upper-division course with no textbook)**

Instructor name:
Office hours:
Instructor contact info:
Meeting day(s) and time:
Meeting location:
Number of units:

Course description: In our increasingly diverse world, intercultural communication is an urgent necessity, not an option. To help fulfill this exigency, the goal of this class is to heighten sensitivity to and understanding of one's own cultural identifications as well as those of others. In doing so, you will be better equipped to understand changing global discourses about cultural groups and others, and improve communication with individuals or groups who are different from you. This course is designed to provide students with key tools to help them to engage in just and equitable communication.

What students can expect to learn in the course (course learning outcomes):
By the end of this course, you should be able to:

- learn the central concepts and important influences in the field of intercultural communication
- apply and connect theory to everyday lived experiences

- understand how one's culture shapes communication strategies
- apply theory to the experiences of others to better understand how the culture of others shapes your communication strategies
- learn to engage as a more interculturally effective interactant

REQUIRED TEXTS AND READINGS

*All readings are available through our course management system.

COURSE POLICIES

**Your university will likely include many required policies to be included in this section. In addition to these boiler plate policies, we recommend the two following sections:

Diversity, Equity, and Inclusion: This course encourages different perspectives related to such factors as race, sex and gender, ethnicity, sexuality, religion, nationality, abilities, socioeconomic standing, immigration status, and other relevant cultural identities. This course seeks to foster understanding and inclusiveness related to such diverse perspectives, ways of knowing, and ways of communicating. You will learn best by listening to those voices that have historically been silenced, making room for discomfort, and opening yourself up to change. I will foster an anti-racist classroom where we strive for equity and justice for all. This is reflected in our readings, discussions, and other classroom materials.

Participation and Engagement: We will engage the topics presented in this class as a community, with shared goals. This class is designed for active student participation, and engagement is a necessary, important, and required part of this course. Your engagement is what will bring meaning to the information in this class and make this class worthwhile for you and others. Engagement may look like (but is not limited to) any of the following:

- Attending class regularly and choosing to be present
- Completing the reading before class
- Participating in classroom discussions
- Participating in class activities
- Speaking your truth
- Listening actively
- Stepping up or stepping back when it comes to speaking in class
- Applying course concepts to life outside the course

Grading: Insert the scale and explanation for how grades will be determined.

ASSIGNMENTS

Exams—You will demonstrate the knowledge you have gained through two in-class examinations. I will provide study guides and we will have a review in class.

Reading Responses—Choose ten readings throughout the semester for which you prepare a one-page **single-spaced** response. Be succinct and do not go over one page. Your response should answer the following questions:

- What is the argument of the reading(s)? Summarize it in your own words and assess whether you agree with it or not, stating your reasons why.
- What surprised or intrigued you about the readings? What did you learn from the reading?
- What are the larger social implications from the reading(s)?
- How does the reading challenge or support other reading you have done?

I am looking for evidence that you have thoroughly done the reading *and* thought critically about it. Your responses should be printed in 12-point font, double-spaced, and hardcopies are due at the beginning of the class (starting on the second-class period). You must be present and on time to turn in the response.

Intercultural Interaction Paper—Have an intercultural interaction with someone from a culture different than your own, read about that different culture in depth, reflect upon it, and write about it. For this particular assignment, the individual should *not* be a U.S.-born citizen. You can interview someone who is studying abroad, an immigrant to the United States, a visitor/tourist, or a dual citizen. Once you have identified the person you will be interacting with for this assignment, read up about their culture and history ahead of time. Also, consider how people typically learn about the cultural group that this person is from. Be cognizant of any stereotypes. Formulate some questions you want to ask them about their culture and experience. Talk to them or interview them about their culture. Observe their interactions (if spending time with a family or group). The paper should include (1) a detailed description of the experience, (2) a discussion of histories of the group (and any hidden histories), (3) a discussion of how their culture differs from your own and implications for future interactions, (4) attention to social categories that were avowed and ascribed for this person, and (5) definition and application of relevant course concepts. The paper should be four+ pages, typed, double-spaced, 12-pt. font, Times New Roman, with 1-inch margins. When you use information that is not your own (i.e., my lectures, book chapters, academic articles) you must cite it using APA style guidelines. This means citing in text *and* including a reference page. I will be grading on your ability to define and apply course concepts in addition to structure, grammar, and clarity of arguments.

Final Application Paper—The major writing assignment of the semester asks you to critically reflect on what you have learned about communication and culture. All options will be graded on your ability to define and apply a variety of course concepts. I am looking for depth in your analysis and a clear understanding of our classroom discussions. This paper should be eight+ full pages in length, typed, double-spaced, 12 pt. font, Times New Roman, with 1-inch margins. When you use information that is not your own (i.e., my lectures, book chapters, academic articles) you must cite it using APA style guidelines. This means citing in text *and* including a reference page. You will choose from one of the following options:

Option 1: Describe an intercultural experience/transition that you have had. It could include (a) a sojourn, (b) a migration, or (c) exploring what it means to have an intercultural relationship/alliance by using your personal experiences as an example. You will need to describe the intercultural experience (including your feelings) and then apply relevant concepts such as (but not limited to) (a) intercultural adaptation, (b) conflict management, (c) social identity, or (d) power/privilege. How was your intercultural experience? In order to answer this, you will have to define culture and apply it to your experiences. Apply at least six course concepts to your experience within the paper. Content will be evaluated on both the definition of concepts and application of those concepts to your experience(s). The paper should meet academic writing standards by being free of mechanical and grammatical errors, having a clear thesis, and using a strong structure.

Option 2: Read one of the following books and critically analyze it using course concepts. You may choose from the following list, or propose a book to me *before* you start the paper:

Americanah by Chimamanda Ngozi Adichie
Between the World and Me by Ta-Nehisi Coates
The Color of Water by James McBride
The Spirit Catches You and You Fall Down: A Hmong Child, Her American Doctors, and the Collision of Two Cultures by Anne Fadiman
The Namesake by Jhumpa Lahiri
Hunger of Memory by Richard Rodriguez
Dreaming in Cuban by Cristina Garcia
The Joy Luck Club by Amy Tan

After reading the book, analyze the text using at least six course concepts. The paper should do the following: (1) Include a summary of the story; (2) provide a description of what you learned about the culture(s) being explored in the text; (3) utilize course concepts to better understand and break down the text. These might include a description of identities (and social categories), stereotypes, positions of power and privilege, and so on; (4) be reflexive and consider the role you play in researching, experiencing, and understanding culture. Describe your reactions to the literature, also considering ethnocentrism. What about the intercultural literature makes you feel (un)comfortable, (un)certain, angry, or otherwise? In what ways might your bias and previous experiences influence your reading and skew your analysis?

Option 3: Submit a proposal for a related topic of your choice. I reserve the right to reject your proposal.

Course schedule: Assigned readings and major writing (or other types of) assignments with due dates.

Table 1. Appendix 10—Example of Syllabus without a Textbook

Week	Date	Topic	Reading
1	T	Course Overview	
	Th	Defining Intercultural Communication	
2	T	Tracing the History of Intercultural Communication	Leeds-Hurwitz (1990), "Notes in the history of intercultural communication"
	Th	Cont.	Moon (2010), "Critical reflections on culture and critical intercultural communication"
3	T	Identity/Subjectivity	Nicotera, Clinkscales, Dorsey, & Niles (2009), "Race as a political identity"
	Th	Power and Privilege	McIntosh (1990), "White privilege: Unpacking the invisible knapsack" Warren (2010), "It really isn't about you"
4	T	Film: Cracking the Codes	
	Th	Histor(ies) and Intercultural Communication	Martin & Nakayama (2013), "Chapter 4"
5	T	Liminality and Borderlands	Leonard (2012), "Struggling for identity: Multiethnic and biracial individuals in America"
	Th		Lawless (2012), "More than white: Locating an invisible class identity"
6	T	Immigration and Intercultural Transitions	Ono (2013), "Understanding immigration and communication"
	Th	Film: Harvest of Empire	
7	T	Case Studies: Analyzing Immigration Rhetoric	Morrisey (2013), "A DREAM disrupted"
	Th	**Exam #1**	
8	T	**Spring Break—No Class**	
	Th	**Spring Break—No Class**	
9	T	Language and Difference	Thurlow (2010), "Speaking of difference: Language, inequality and interculturality"
	Th		Tsuda (2010), "Speaking against the hegemony of English"

(Continued)

Table 1. (Continued)

Week	Date	Topic	Reading
10	T	Intercultural Alliances	Allen (2012), "Sapphire and Sappho: Allies in authenticity"
	Th		Lawless (2016), "Ally, friend, or mentor?"
11	T	Intercultural Relationships	Halualani (2010), "Intercultural interactions at a multicultural university"
	Th		Foeman & Nance (2002), "Building new cultures"
12	T	Globalization and Intercultural Communication	Shome and Hegde (2002), "Culture, communication, & the challenge of globalization"
	Th		Sorrells (2010), "Re-imagining intercultural communication in the context of globalization"
13	T	Critical Departures in Intercultural Communication	Halualani & Nakayama (2010), "Critical intercultural communication studies: At a crossroads"
	Th		Chavez (2013): "Pushing boundaries: Queer intercultural communication"
14	T	Effective Intercultural Communication and Future Directions	Martin & Nakayama (2013), "Chapter 12: Striving for engaged and effective intercultural communication"
	Th		Lawless & Chen, "Still a Sensitive Subject?"
15	T	Review and Course Wrap-Up	
	Th	Exam 2	

LIST OF READINGS

Allen, B. J. (2012). Sapphire and Sappho: Allies in authenticity. In A. González, M. Houston, & V. Chen (Eds.). *Our voices: Essays in culture, ethnicity, and communication* (pp. 197–201). New York, NY: Oxford.

Chávez, K. (2013). Pushing boundaries: Queer intercultural communication. *Journal of International and Intercultural Communication*, 6(2), 83–95.

Foeman, A., & Nance, T. (2002). Building new cultures, reframing old images: Success strategies of interracial couples. *The Howard Journal of Communications, 13*, 237–249. doi:10.1080/10646170290109716

Halualani, R. T. (2010). Intercultural interactions at a multicultural university: Students' definitions and sensemakings of intercultural interaction. *Journal of International and Intercultural Communication*, 3(4), 304–324.

Halualani, R. T., & Nakayama, T. K. (2010). Critical intercultural communication studies: At a crossroads. In T. K. Nakayama & R. T. Halualani (Eds.), *The handbook of critical intercultural communication* (pp. 1–16). West Sussex, UK: Wiley-Blackwell.

Lawless, B. (2012). More than white: Locating an invisible class identity. In A. González, M. Houston, & V. Chen (Eds.). *Our voices: Essays in culture, ethnicity, and communication* (pp. 247–253). New York, NY: Oxford.

Lawless, B. (2016). Ally, friend, or mentor? Creating and maintaining effective cross-class alliances. *Journal of International and Intercultural Communication*, *9*(4), 334–350. doi:10.1080/17513057.2016.1225443

Lawless, B., & Chen, Y.-W. (2020). Still a "sensitive" subject? Unpacking strengths and struggles of intercultural communication pedagogies. *Howard Journal of Communications*, 1–16. doi:10.1080/10646175.2019.1707135

Leeds-Hurwitz, W. (1990). Notes in the history of intercultural communication: The Foreign Service Institute and the mandate for intercultural training. *Quarterly Journal of Speech*, *76*, 262–281.

Leonard, M. F. (2012). Struggling for identity: Multiethnic and biracial individuals in America. In A. González, M. Houston, & V. Chen (Eds.), *Our voices: Essays in culture, ethnicity, and communication* (pp. 216–229). New York, NY: Oxford.

Martin, J. N., & Nakayama, T. K. (2013). *Intercultural communication in contexts* (6th ed.). New York, NY: McGraw Hill.

McIntosh, P. (1990). White privilege: Unpacking the invisible knapsack. Retrieved August 16, 2020, from http://www.cwru.edu/president/aaction/UnpackingThe Knapsack.pdf

Moon, D. G. (2010). Critical reflections on culture and critical intercultural communication. In T. K. Nakayama & R. T. Halualani (Eds.), *The handbook of critical intercultural communication* (pp. 33–52). West Sussex, UK: Wiley-Blackwell.

Morrisey, M. (2013). A DREAM disrupted: Undocumented migrant youth disidentifications with U.S. citizenship. *Journal of International and Intercultural Communication*, *6*(2), 145–162.

Nicotera, A. M., Clinkscales, M. J., Dorsey, L. K., & Niles, M. N. (2009). Race as political identity: Problematic issues for applied communication research. In L. R. Frey and K. N. Cissna (Eds.), *Routledge handbook of applied communication research* (pp. 203–218). New York, NY: Routledge.

Ono, K. A. (2013). Understanding immigration and communication contextually and interpersonally. In N. Bardhan & M. P. Orbe (Eds.), *Identity research and communication: Intercultural reflections and future directions* (pp. 149–164). Lanham, MD: Lexington Books

Shome, R., & Hegde, R. (2002). Communication and the challenge of globalization. *Critical Studies in Media Communication*, *19*, 172–189.

Sorrells, K. (2010). Re-imagining intercultural communication in the context of globalization. In T. K Nakayama & R. T. Halualani (Eds.), *The handbook of critical intercultural communication* (pp. 171–189). West Sussex, UK: Wiley-Blackwell.

Thurlow, C. (2010). Speaking of difference: Language, inequality and interculturality. In T. K Nakayama & R. T. Halualani (Eds.), *The handbook of critical intercultural communication* (pp. 227–247). West Sussex, UK: Wiley-Blackwell.

Tsuda, Y. (2010). Speaking against the hegemony of English: Problems, ideologies, and solutions. In T. K Nakayama & R. T. Halualani (Eds.), *The handbook of critical intercultural communication* (pp. 248–269). West Sussex, UK: Wiley-Blackwell.

Warren, J. T. (2010). "It really isn't about you": Whiteness and the dangers of thinking you got it. In T. K. Nakayama & R. T. Halualani (Eds.), *The Handbook of Critical Intercultural Communication* (pp. 446–460). West Sussex, UK: Wiley-Blackwell.

Appendix I

Challenging Microaggressions: What Would You Do?

Read each of the following scenarios. With a partner, explain the *denotative* and *connotative* meanings that emerge from what is being said. In other words, how does the literal statement differ from alternative meanings that are imbued in each scenario? After differentiating between denotative and connotative meanings, apply the C.H.A.N.G.E. model to the scenario. How can these microaggressions be combatted?

C = **Communicate** with others about microaggressions

H = **Hear** others when they say they have been microaggressed

A = **Acknowledge** when you perpetuate microaggressions and experience them

N = **Negotiate** differences in understanding microaggressions

G = **Grow** awareness of the social/cultural impact of microaggressions in society

E = **Engage** in difficult conversations that will help to end microaggressive behaviors

---

SCENARIO 1

David is taking a service-learning class, in which he does tutoring hours with low-income students at a nearby elementary school. He is assigned to work with Andrés, a six-year-old first grader whose first language is Spanish. David, struggling to pronounce Andrés says, "Let's just call you Andy. That's easier for everyone." Andrés feels uncomfortable but doesn't want to disappoint his new mentor. He obliges but later tells the program director what happened.

SCENARIO 2

Vijaya, an Indian woman, is sitting in the faculty lounge, chatting with a few of her colleagues. The janitor comes in and says, "Something smells weird in the fridge. Is it yours?" while looking at Vijaya. Her colleagues don't say anything and she frustratingly tells the janitor, "No. It's not mine. Why do you ask?"

SCENARIO 3

Paul, a gay college student, sits in the front row of his Biology lecture. The professor is discussing the biology of attraction. He turns to Paul and says, "What attracts you to women?" Paul embarrassingly says, "Um, I don't know . . ." His professor reminds Paul that participation is part of his grade. Paul makes up an answer to comply with his professor and avoid outing himself to the 200+ students in the lecture hall.

SCENARIO 4

Shawn identifies as transgender and uses the pronouns he/him. His professor frequently refers to Shawn as "she" or "her," despite being corrected. The professor apologizes but does not correct his behavior in future encounters.

Appendix J

What is an ally? What is a friend? How are they different? How are they different? Describe the characteristics for each. Are there any that overlap?

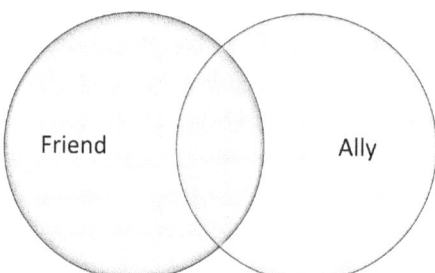

Friend and Ally Venn Diagram.

Describe an ideal intercultural alliance below. Give an example of who might be involved in the relationship and how each party would have to communicate in order to build an alliance. Refer back to the three characteristics of an intercultural alliance discussed in class. ☺

Appendix K

Alliance Reflection Paper

This four- to five-page paper asks you to apply course readings and discussion in order to evaluate a particular intercultural alliance in your life (or the potential for one). Identify how the relationship is/could be an intercultural alliance (recognition of history, recognition of power/privilege, orientation of affirmation). Describe how the relationship has been successful and/or how it might be improved. To do this, you will need to apply major topics covered in our course such as: approaches to culture and intercultural communication, relationship development, approaches to conflict resolution, attention to contextual factors, approach to power and status, and use of intercommunity dialogue and peacebuilding strategies.

IN ORDER TO SUCCESSFULLY WRITE THIS PAPER, YOU WILL NEED TO ACCOMPLISH THE FOLLOWING:

(1) Demonstrate your knowledge of intercultural alliances by presenting a definition and utilizing course materials in your description of an alliance.
(2) Describe what an intercultural alliance looks like for you (extend Collier's three components) based on class readings and discussion.
(3) Begin to explore your own levels of privilege/disadvantage on various levels. Consider intersectionality.
(4) Contemplate how history and context(s) have influenced this relationship.
(5) Describe the challenges with/in the relationship and how (if at all) you have overcome them, or how you might consider doing so in the future.

Appendix L

Alliance Dialogues

Jane: So, last week I gave you the task of calling the unemployment office with the task of better understanding how you go about a new job search. Did you accomplish that?

Maria: No, I just didn't get around to it.

Jane: Ok, well what about calling the Head Start pre-school to check on prices?

Maria: It has just been a really busy week since Sadie was sick, and we don't have health insurance, and I had to stay home with her . . . lots of stuff came up.

Jane: Well, that's life, Maria. You have to handle it all. Every week I come in here and tell you what can help you, but it seems like you don't listen. I have better things to do than give advice that won't be taken! Only you have the power to change your situation, Maria. Pull yourself up by the bootstraps.

Maria: Yea, I know. I'm sorry.

Gloria: I'm going to coach you through the interview process. I really want you to do well!

Naudia: Thanks, I'm just real nervous.

Gloria: You're "really" nervous. I hope you're more cognizant of your language when you go in there. You not only need to dress to impress, but remember what you learned about the formal register of language.

Naudia: So, don't be myself?

Gloria: I didn't say that, honey. I just want you to be the best that you can be. And grammar and enunciation are part of that. You have to present yourself well. I did that and look where I am now!

Appendix M

Observing Your Communit(ies)

Objectives: (1) Understand how your perception of the city you live (or attend school) in is socially constructed. (2) Uncover new ways of understanding community/communities based on cultural observation.

Background: Most cities are made up of neighborhoods, smaller communities, or microcosms that segregate people by race, socioeconomic status, sexuality, or some other social stratification. For example, in San Francisco, CA, the Marina neighborhood has an average home price of $2.4 million. Meanwhile, the Tenderloin neighborhood is known as the poorest area, with a large homeless population. The Castro neighborhood is known as a microcosm of LGBTQ members—especially white gay men.

In order to work toward justice in our communities, we must first understand the cultural groups that make up our communities and the inequities that are experienced by different cultural groups. This can be achieved through observation.

Assignment: The class will be split into four to six groups. Each group will be assigned a single neighborhood to observe for a minimum of two hours. While doing field work in this neighborhood, find a place that you can easily settle in and observe.

- Find a spot or spots to observe. While you may want to sit and people watch, you'll also find that walking around can be useful in your observation.
- Observe the space. What do the buildings look like? What do the streets look like? What public spaces are available? What businesses are a part of the community? What necessities (e.g., groceries) are easily accessible? How are food/groceries/other commodities priced?

- Observe who enters this space. What do people look like? Where are they going? What are they doing? Who are they with? What are they wearing? What is their mood?
- Listen to communication. What is being communicated both verbally and nonverbally in this space? Is this space for recreation, business, personal, residential, or other uses?
- What is your sense of the social stratification of this neighborhood? Who is *allowed* to be a part of this community? What issues face this community?

Debrief: After each group observes a part of the city, we will spend time in class sharing our observations and comparing the sub-communities we observed. We'll then answer the following questions:

- What do the observations have in common? How do they differ?
- What historical context informs the development and/or disparity of this community?
- What injustices and inequities become visible through these observations and comparisons?
- How can intercultural communication be used to intervene in these injustices?

Appendix N

Mentoring Map for Intercultural Instructors

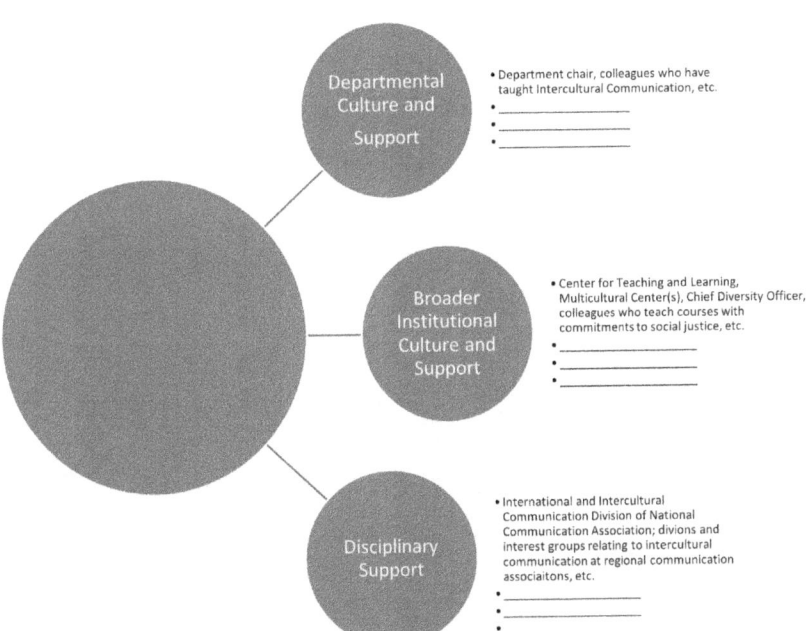

Support Circle Diagram. Note: This is inspired by NCFDD Mentoring Map from National Center for Faculty Development and Diversity: https://www.insidehighered.com/sites/default/server_files/files/Mentoring%20Map%5B1%5D(1).pdf

Glossary

Afrocentricity a philosophical stance that starts with and centralizes African agency, interests, values, and worldviews

Ascription patterns and processes of how one's own group, or groups, is/are communicated and represented by others

Asiacentricity an approach to knowledge and theory-building through centralizing Asian experiences through languages, religious-philosophical traditions, and historical struggles

Avowal patterns, negotiations, and processes of how an individual represents himself/herself/themselves to others as a group member or a member of multiple groups

Colorblindness an ideology assuming that racism is a thing of the past, and race and racialization no longer matter

Critical Intercultural Communication Pedagogy pedagogical beliefs and practices that correspond to, reflect, and hold critical intercultural communication studies accountable in the classroom

Diversity a neoliberal term that commonly evokes difference (e.g., race, gender, class, nationality) without a political commitment to action and is often used to reproduce race-based and intersectional group stereotypes

Equity can be understood as "a standard for judging whether a state of affairs is just or unjust" and fair or unfair, and often works to keep the focus on equitable outcomes for minority group members in response to differential histories of discriminations (Dowd & Bensimon, 2015, p. 9)

Ideology a dominant yet often invisible and/or taken-for-granted belief and value system

Inclusion can function either similarly to (a) diversity in paying lip service to which groups and group members are present, included, or welcomed at an institution; or (b) more politically aligned with equity in ensuring that voices and experiences of minoritized group members matter in an institution's decision-making across levels in response to histories of racism, sexism, classism, and more

Intersectionality first coined by Kimberlé Williams Crenshaw to analyze and theorize lived experiences that embody multiple standpoints of domination such as race and gender interlock

Microaggressions brief and common verbal, nonverbal, or environmental messages that communicate, whether intentionally or unintentionally, indignity, rudeness, hostility, or direct attack targeted at members of minoritized and historically marginalized groups

Neoliberalism the universalization, extension, and dissemination of market values and enterprise logic to all institutions and social actions

Neoliberal multiculturalism active recruitment of diverse bodies without providing the resources needed to succeed

Racialization a process by which skin color, and/or any relevant physical-phenotypical attribute, signifies and communicates social, cultural, or political significance

Social justice both a goal and a process of co-creating spaces for individuals and groups to speak their truths on their own terms and be heard; a goal and a process of relentlessly striving for equitable distribution of and access to resources; a goal and process of persisting to recognize and challenge power imbalances that organize everyday communication interactions; and a goal and a process of practicing actions to bring about positive changes in society

White supremacy the belief in the "natural" and inherent superiority of whites as a racial group over groups and people of color

Notes

INTRODUCTION

1. See professorwatchlist.com for examples.

5. COMMUNITY ENGAGEMENT FOR SOCIAL JUSTICE

1. Community-engaged learning is sometimes referred to as *service-learning*. Many programs are moving away from "service-learning" designations in order to emphasize working *with* community, rather than a top-down service orientation of "I've come here to help."

2. See, for example, organizations like Campus Reform, whose goal is to expose liberal bias on campus.

References

Adams, M., Bell, L. A., Goodman, D. J., & Joshi, K. Y. (Eds.). (2016). *Teaching for diversity and social justice* (3rd ed.). New York, NY: Routledge.

Adams, M., & Zúñiga, X. (2018). Core concepts for social justice education. In M. Adams, W. J. Blumenfeld, D. C. J. Catalano, K. S. DeJong, H. W. Hackman, L. E. Hopkins, B. J. Love, M. L. Peters, D. Shlasko, & X. Zúñiga (Eds.), *Readings for diversity and social justice* (4th ed., pp. 41–49). New York, NY: Routledge.

Adichie, C. N. (2009). The danger of a single story. *TED Talk*. Retrieved from https://www.youtube.com/watch?v=D9Ihs241zeg

Ahmed, S. (2007). The language of diversity. *Ethnic and Racial Studies, 30*(2), 235–256. doi:10.1080/01419870601143927

Alcoff, L. M. (1991). The problem of speaking for others. *Cultural Critique, 20*, 5–32. Retrieved from https://www.jstor.org/stable/1354221?seq=1

Alexander, A., & Liu, M. (2018). "Be the change you want to see": A three-part semester-long assignment in an interracial communication class. *Communication Teacher, 32*(4), 225–230. doi:10.1080/17404622.2017.1372789

Alexander, B. K., Arasaratnam, L. A., Durham, A., Flores, L., Leeds-Hurwitz, W., Mendoza, S. L., . . . Halualani, R. (2014). Defining and communicating what "intercultural" and "intercultural communication" means to us. *Journal of International and Intercultural Communication, 7*(1), 14–37. doi:10.1080/17513057.2014.869524

Alexander, B. K., Arasaratnam, L. A., Flores, L. A., Leeds-Hurwitz, W., Mendoza, S. L., Oetzel, J., . . . Halualani, R. T. (2014). Our role as intercultural scholars, practitioners, activists, and teachers in addressing these key intercultural urgencies, issues, and challenges. *Journal of International and Intercultural Communication, 7*(1), 68–99. doi:10.1080/17513057.2014.869526

Allen, B. J. (2011). *Difference matters: Communicating social identity* (2nd ed.). Long Grove, IL: Waveland Press.

References

Allen, B. J. (2012). Sapphire and Sappho: Allies in authenticity. In A. González, M. Houston, & V. Chen (Eds.), *Our voices: Essays in culture, ethnicity, and communication* (5th ed., pp. 197–201). New York, NY: Oxford.

Allen, B. J., Broome, B. J., Jones, T. S., Chen, V., & Collier, M. J. (2003). Intercultural alliances: A cyber dialogue among scholars-practitioners. In M. J. Collier (Ed.), *Intercultural Alliances: Critical Transformation* (Vol. 25, pp. 249–319). Thousand Oaks, CA: SAGE.

Allen, R. L. (2001). The globalization of white supremacy: Toward a critical discourse on the racialization of the world. *Educational Theory*, *51*(4), 467–485.

Anderson, B. (1983). *Imagined communities: Reflections on the origin and spread of nationalism.* London, UK: Verso.

Antony, M. G. (2016). Exploring diversity through dialogue: Avowed and ascribed identities. *Communication Teacher*, *30*(3), 125–130. doi:10.1080/17404622.2016.1192663

Appadurai, A. (1996). *Modernity at large: Cultural dimensions of globalization*. Minneapolis: University of Minnesota Press.

Asante, G. (2016). Glocalized whiteness: Sustaining and reproducing whiteness through "skin toning" in post-colonial Ghana. *Journal of International and Intercultural Communication*, *9*(2), 87–103. doi:10.1080/17513057.2016.1154184

Asante, M. K. (1980/1998). *The Afrocentric idea: Revised and expanded edition.* Philadelphia, PA: Temple University Press.

Ashby-King, D. T., & Hanasono, L. K. (2019). Diverging discourses: Examining how college students majoring in communication define diversity. *Qualitative Research Reports in Communication*. doi:10.1080/17459435.2019.1572645

Atay, A. (2015). *Globalization's impact on cultural identity formation: Queer diasporic males in Cyberspace.* Lanham, MD: Lexington Books.

Atay, A., & Toyosaki, S. (2018). *Critical intercultural communication pedagogy.* Lanham, MD: Lexington Books.

Backlund, P., Detwiler, T. J., Arneson, P., & Danielson, M. A. (2010). Assessing communication knowledge, skills, and attitudes. In P. Backland & G. Wakefield (Eds.), *A communication assessment primer* (pp. 1–14). Washington, DC: National Communication Association. Retrieved from https://www.natcom.org/sites/default/files/pages/Assessment_Resources_A_Communication_Assessment_Primer.pdf

Baldwin, J. R., Coleman, R. R. M., González, A., & Shenoy-Packer, S. (2014). *Intercultural communication for everyday life*. Malden, MA: Wiley Blackwell.

Bardhan, N., & Orbe, M. P. (2012). Introduction: Identity research in intercultural communication. In N. Bardhan & M. P. Orbe (Eds.), *Identity research and communication: Intercultural reflections and future directions* (pp. xiii–xxv). Lanham, MD: Lexington Books.

Bertelsen, D. A., & Goodboy, A. K. (2009). Curriculum planning: Trends in communication studies, workplace competencies, and current programs at 4-year colleges and universities. *Communication Education*, *58*, 262–275. doi:10.1080/03634520902755458

Blithe, S. J. (2016). Teaching intercultural communication through service-learning. *Communication Teacher*, *30*(3), 165–701. doi:10.1080/17404622.2016.1192666

Bloom, B. S. (1956). *Taxonomy of educational objectives: The classification of educational goals*. New York, NY: Longmans, Green.

Boler, M. (1999). *Feeling power: Emotions and education*. New York, NY: Routledge.

Boler, M. (2014). Teaching for hope: The ethics of shattering worldviews. In V. Bozalek, B. Leibowtiz, R. Carolissen, & M. Boler (Eds.), *Discerning critical hope in educational practices* (pp. 26–39). New York, NY: Routledge.

Borden, A. W. (2007). The impact of service-learning on ethnocentrism in an intercultural communication course. *Journal of Experiential Education, 30*(2), 171–183. doi:10.1177/105382590703000206

Boyle-Baise, M. (2002). *Multicultural service learning: Educating teachers in diverse communities*. New York, NY: Teachers College Press.

Calafell, B. M. (2010). When will we all matter? Exploring race, pedagogy, and sustained hope for the academy. In D. L. Fassett & J. T. Warren (Eds.), *The SAGE handbook of communication and instruction* (pp. 343–359). Thousand Oaks, CA: SAGE.

Calafell, B. M. (2015). *Monstrosity, performance, and race in contemporary culture*. New York, NY: Peter Lang.

Carrillo Rowe, A. M. (2003). Bridge inscriptions: Transracial feminist alliances, possibilities, and foreclosures. In M. J. Collier (Ed.), *Intercultural Alliances: Critical Transformation* (Vol. 25, pp. 49–80). Thousand Oaks, CA: SAGE.

Carrillo Rowe, A. M. (2008). *Power lines: On the subject of feminist alliances*. Durham, NC: Duke University Press.

Carrillo Rowe, A. M. (2010). Entering the inter: Power lines in intercultural communication. In T. K. Nakayama & R. T. Halualani (Eds.), *The Handbook of Critical Intercultural Communication* (pp. 216–226). Malden, MA: Wiley-Blackwell.

Carrillo Rowe, A., & Malhotra, S. (2007). (Un)hinging whiteness. In L. Cooks & J. S. Simpson (Eds.), *Whiteness, pedagogy, performance: Dis/placing race* (pp. 271–298). Lanham, MD: Lexington Books.

Chen, G.-M. (2012). The impact of new media on intercultural communication in global context. *China Media Research, 8*(2), 1–10.

Chen, Y.-W. (2014a). "Are you an immigrant?": Identity-based critical reflections of teaching intercultural communication. In K. G. Hendrix & A. Hebbani (Eds.), *Hidden roads: Nonnative English-speaking international professors in the classroom* (pp. 5–16). *New Directions for Teaching and Learning, 138*, San Francisco, CA: Jossey-Bass. doi:10.1002/tl.20091

Chen, Y.-W. (2014b). Public engagement exercises with racial and cultural "others": Some thoughts, questions, and considerations. *Journal of Public Deliberation, 10*(1), article 14. Retrieved from: http://www.publicdeliberation.net/jpd/vol10/iss1/Chen, Y.-W. (2018). "Why don't you speak (up), Asian/immigrant/woman?": Rethink silence and voice through family oral history. *Departures in Critical Qualitative Research, 7*(2), 29–48. doi:10.1525/dcqr.2018.7.2.29

Chen, Y.-W., & Lawless, B. (2018). "Oh my god! You have become so Americanized": Paradoxes of adaptation and strategic ambiguity among female immigrant faculty. *Journal of International and Intercultural Communication, 11*(1), 1–20. doi:10.1080/17513057.2017.1385825

Chen, Y.-W., & Lawless, B. (2019). Teaching critical moments within neoliberal universities: Exploring critical intercultural communication pedagogy. *Journal of Intercultural Communication Research*, *48*(5), 553–573. doi:10.1080/17475759.2019.1683056

Chen, Y.-W., Simmons, N., & Kang, D. (2015). "My family isn't racist—however...": Multiracial/Multicultural Obama-ism as an ideological barrier to teaching intercultural communication. *Journal of International and Intercultural Communication*, *8*(2), 167–186. doi:10.1080/17513057.2015.1025331

Cheng, H.-I. (2008). *Culturing interface: Identity, communication, and Chinese transnationalism*. New York, NY: Peter Lang.

Clemens, C. (2017). Ally or accomplice? The language of activism. *Teaching Tolerance*. Retrieved from https://www.tolerance.org/magazine/ally-or-accomplice-the-language-of-activismCollier, M. J. (1998). Intercultural friendships as interpersonal alliances. In J. Martin, T. Nakayama, & L. Flores (Eds.) *Readings in cultural contexts* (pp. 370–368). Mountain View, CA: Mayfield Publishing.

Collier, M. J. (2002). *Transforming communication about culture: Critical new directions*. Thousand Oaks, CA: SAGE.

Collier, M. J. (2003). Negotiating intercultural alliance relationships: Toward transformation. In M. J. Collier (Ed.), *Intercultural alliances: Critical transformation* (Vol. 25, pp. 1–16). Thousand Oaks, CA: SAGE.

Collier, M. J. (2005). Theorizing cultural identifications: Critical updates and continuing evolution. In W. B Gudykunst (Ed.), *Theorizing about intercultural communication* (pp. 235–256). Thousand Oaks, CA: SAGE.

Collier, M. J. (2014). *Dancing with difference: Community engagement and intercultural praxis*. New York, NY: Peter Lang.

Collier, M. J., & Ringera, K. (2016). Intercultural allies dancing with difference: International Peace Initiatives, Kenya. In K. Sorrells & S. Sekimoto (Eds.), *Globalizing intercultural communication: A reader* (pp. 155–166). Los Angeles, CA: SAGE.

Collier, M. J., & Thomas, M. (1988). Cultural identity. In Y. Y. Kim & W. B. Gudykunst (Eds.), *Theories of intercultural communication* (pp. 99–120). Newbury Park, CA: SAGE.

Collins, P. H. (2000). *Black feminist thought: Knowledge, consciousness, and the politics of empowerment*. New York, NY: Routledge.

Cooks, L. (2001). From distance and uncertainty to research and pedagogy in the borderlands: Implications for the future of intercultural communication. *Communication Theory*, *11*(3), 339–351.

Cooks, L. (2017). Intercultural communication, ethics, and activism pedagogy. In A. Atay & S. Toyosaki (Eds.), *Critical intercultural communication pedagogy* (pp. 27–46). Lanham, MD: Lexington Books.

Cooks, L., & Simpson, J. S. (Eds.). (2007). *Whiteness, pedagogy, performance: Dis/Placing race*. Lanham, MD: Lexington Books.

Cote, J. E., & Levine, C. G. (2002). *Identity formation, agency, and culture: A social psychological synthesis*. Mahwah, NJ: Lawrence Erlbaum.

Covarrubias, P. O. (2008). Masked silence sequences: Hearing discrimination in the college classroom. *Communication, Culture and Critique*, *1*(3), 227–252. doi:10.1111/j.1753-9137.2008.00021.x

Craig, R. T. (2007). Issue forum introduction: Cultural bias in communication theory. *Communication Monographs, 74*(2), 256–258. doi:10.1080/03637750701390101

Crenshaw, K. (1991). Mapping the margins: Intersectionality, identity politics, and violence against women of color. *Stanford Law Review, 43*(6), 1241–1299.

Darder, A. (2012). Neoliberalism in the academic borderlands: An on-going struggle for equality and human rights. *Education Studies, 48*, 412–426. doi:10.1080/00131946.2012.714334

Davis, R. W., & Patterson-Masuka, A. (2015). *Intercultural communication for global engagement*. Dubuque, IA: Kendall Hunt.

De Leon, N. (2014). Developing intercultural competence by participating in intensive intercultural service-learning. *Michigan Journal of Community Service Learning, 21*(1), 17–30.

Denzin, N. K. (2010). *The qualitative manifesto: A call to arms*. New York, NY: Routledge.

DeTurk, S. (2006). The power of dialogue: Consequences of intergroup dialogue and their implications for agency and alliance building. *Communication Quarterly, 54*(1), 33–51. doi: 10.1080/01463370500270355

DeTurk, S. (2011). Allies in action: The communicative experiences of people who challenge social injustice on behalf of others. *Communication Quarterly, 59*(5), 569–590. doi: 10.1080/01463373.2011.614209

DeTurk, S. (2015). *Activism, alliance building, and the Esperanza Peace and Justice Center*. Lanham, MD: Lexington Books.

DiAngelo, R. (2018). *White fragility: Why it's so hard for white people to talk about racism*. Boston, MA: Beacon Press.

Domosh, M. (2006). *American commodities in an age of empire*. New York, NY: Routledge.

Dowd, A. C., & Bensimon, E. M. (2015). *Engaging the "race question": Accountability and equity in U.S. higher education*. New York, NY: Teachers College Press.

Drabinski, K. (2011). Identity matters: Teaching transgender in the women's studies classroom. *Radical Teacher, 92*, 10–20. doi:10.1353/rdt.2011.0042

Duffy, L. N., Mowatt, R. A., Fuchs, M., & Salisbury, M. A. (2014). Making diversity tangible: Assessing the role of service learning in teaching diversity and social justice. *International Journal of Critical Pedagogy, 5*(2), 54–75.

Eguchi, S. (2011). Cross-national identity transformation: Becoming a gay "Asian-American" man. *Sexuality & Culture, 15*, 19–40. doi:10.1007/s12119-010-9080-z

Endres, D., & Gould, M. (2009). "I am also in the position to use my whiteness to help them out": The communication of whiteness in service learning. *Western Journal of Communication, 73*(4), 418–436. doi:10.1080/10570310903279083

Fassett, D. L., & Warren, J. T. (2007). *Critical communication pedagogy*. Thousand Oaks, CA: SAGE.

Files-Thompson, N., & McConatha, M. (2020). Mobilizing allies for Black transgender women: Digital stories, intersectionality, and #SayHerName. In S. Eguchi & B. M. Calafell (Eds.), *Queer intercultural communication: The intersectional politics of belonging in and across differences* (pp. 239–257). Lanham, MD: Rowman & Littlefield.

Flores, L. A. (2003). Constructing rhetorical borders: Peons, illegal aliens, and competing narratives of immigration. *Critical Studies in Media Communication, 20*(4), 362–387. doi:10.1080/0739318032000142025

Foucault, M. (1972). *The archaeology of knowledge and the discourse on language* (A. M. Sheridan Smith, Trans.). New York, NY: Routledge.

Freire, P. (1970). *Pedagogy of the oppressed*. New York, NY: Continuum.

French Jr., J. R. P., & Raven, B. (1959). The bases of social power. In D. Cartwright (Ed.), *Studies in social power* (pp. 150–167). Ann Arbor, MI: The University of Michigan.

Frey, L. R., & Palmer, D. L. (2014). Introduction: Teaching communication activism. In L. R. Frey & D. L. Palmer (Eds.), *Teaching communication activism: Communication education for social justice* (pp. 1–42). New York, NY: Hampton Press.

Frey, L. R., & Palmer, D. L. (2017). Communication activism pedagogy and research: Communication education scholarship to promote social justice. *Communication Education, 66*(3), 362–367. doi:10.1080/03634523.2017.1290812

Giddens, A. (1979). *Central problems in social theory: Action, structure and contradiction in social analysis*. Berkeley and Los Angeles: University of California Press.

Goodman, D. J. (2010). Difficult dialogues. *College Teaching, 43*(2), 47–52.

Griffin, R. A. (2012). Navigating the politics of identity/identities and exploring the promise of critical love. In N. Bardhan & M. P. Orbe (Eds.), *Identity research and communication: Intercultural reflections and future directions* (pp. 207–221). Lanham, MD: Lexington Books.

Griffin, R. A. (2015). Problematic representations of strategic whiteness and "post-racial" pedagogy: A critical intercultural reading of *The Help*. *Journal of International and Intercultural Communication, 8*(2), 147–166. doi:10.1080/17513057.2015.1025330

Halualani, R. T., Mendoza, S. L., & Drzewiecka, J. A. (2009). "Critical" junctures in intercultural communication studies: A review. *The Review of Communication, 9*(1), 17–35. doi:10.1080/15358590802169504

Halualani, R. T., & Nakayama T. K. (2010). Critical intercultural communication studies: At a crossroads. In Nakayama, T. K, & Halualani, R. T. (Eds.), *The handbook of critical intercultural communication* (pp. 1–16). Malden, MA: Wiley-Blackwell.

Hanasono, L. K. (2016). Making a difference: A community-based campaign that promotes diversity and inclusion. *Communication Teacher, 31*(1), 27–34. doi: 10.1080/17404622.2016.1244348

Harris, T. M., & Moffitt, K. (2019). Centering communication in our understanding of microaggressions, race, and otherness in academe and beyond. *Southern Communication Journal, 84*(2), 67–71. doi:10.1080/1041794X.2018.1515978

Hecht, M. L., Jackson, R. L., & Pitts, M. J. (2005). Culture: Intersections of intergroup and identity theories. In Harwood, J. & Giles, H. (Eds.), *Intergroup communication: Multiple perspectives* (pp. 21–42). New York, NY: Peter Lang.

Hedley, M., & Markowitz, L. (2001). Avoiding moral dichotomies: Teaching controversial topics to resistant students. *Teaching Sociology, 29*, 195–208.

Hegde, R. (1996). Narratives of silence: Rethinking gender, agency, and power from the communication experiences of battered women in South India. *Communication Studies, 47*(4), 303–317.

Hendrix, K. G., Jackson, R. L., II, & Warren, J. R. (2003). Shifting academic landscapes: Exploring co-identities, identity negotiation, and critical progressive pedagogy. *Communication Education, 52*, 177–190. doi:10.1080/0363452032000156181

Heuman, A. N. (2015). An intercultural partnership for social justice in the Rio Grande Valley TX Colonias. *Journal of International and Intercultural Communication, 8*(3), 193–207. doi:10.1080/17513057.2015.1057916

Holliday, A. (2011). *Intercultural communication and ideology*. Los Angeles, CA: SAGE.

hooks, b. (1990). *Yearning race, gender, and cultural politics*. Boston, MA: South End Press.

hooks, b. (2000). *Where we stand: Class matters*. New York, NY: Routledge.

Houston, M. (2004). "When black women talk with white women: Why the dialogues are difficult." In A. González, M. Houston, & V. Chen (Eds.), *Our voices: Essays in culture, ethnicity, and communication* (4th ed., pp. 119–125). New York, NY: Oxford University Press.

Howard, G. R. (2016). *We can't teach what we don't know: White teachers, multiracial schools*. New York, NY: Teachers College Press.

Howard, T. C. (2003). Culturally relevant pedagogy: Ingredients for critical teacher reflection. *Theory into Practice, 42*(3), 195–202. doi:10.1207/s15430421tip4203_

Johnson, A. G. (2001). *Privilege, power, and difference*. Mountain View, CA: Mayfield Publishing Company.

Johnson, A. G. (2006). *Privilege, power, and difference* (2nd ed.). Boston, MA: McGraw Hill.

Johnson, J. R., & Bhatt, A. J. (2003). Gendered and racialized identities and alliances in the classroom: Formations in/of resistive space. *Communication Education, 52*(3/4), 230–244.

Kahl Jr., D. H. (2013). Critical communication pedagogy and assessment: Reconciling two seemingly incongruous ideas. *International Journal of Communication, 7*, 2610–2630.

Kahl Jr., D. H. (2014). Basic course central student learning outcomes: Enhancing the traditional with the critical. *Basic Communication Course Annual, 26*(9), 34–43.

Kahl Jr, D. H. (2017). Addressing the challenges of critical communication pedagogy scholarship: Moving toward an applied agenda. *Journal of Applied Communication Research, 45*(1), 116–120. doi:10.1080/00909882.2016.1248468

Kahl Jr., D. H. (2018). Creating critical objectives and assessments using a critical communication pedagogical framework. *Communication Teacher, 32*(1), 36–41. doi:10.1080/17404622.2017.1372792

Kahl Jr., D. H. (2018). Resisting the influence of neoliberalism on millennial faculty through critical communication pedagogy and critical mentoring. In A. Atay & S. Toyosaki (Eds.), *Millennial culture and communication pedagogies: Narratives from the classroom and higher education* (pp. 3–19). Lanham, MD: Lexington Books.

Kawai, Y. (2009). Neoliberalism, nationalism, and intercultural communication: A critical analysis of a Japan's neoliberal nationalism discourse under globalization. *Journal of International and Intercultural Communication, 2*(1), 16–43. doi:10.1080/17513050802567049

Kelly, S., & Davis, M. J. (2011). Just another brick in the wall . . . or not? A paradigm introduction activity. *Communication Teacher, 4,* 222–227. doi:10.1080/17404622.2011.601724

Kendi, I. X. (2019). *How to be an antiracist.* New York, NY: One World.

Kennerly, R. M. (with Davis, T.). (2014). Service-learning, intercultural communication, and video production praxis: Developing a sustainable program of community activism with/in a Latino/a migrant community. In L. R. Frey & D. L. Palmer (Eds.), *Teaching communication activism: Communication education for social justice* (pp. 321–352). New York, NY: Hampton Press.

Kerber, A. (2020). Using "The Phone at the End of the World" to analyze diverse arguments on globalization. *Communication Teacher, 34*(2), 114–117. doi:10.1080/17404622.2019.1614205

Kuehl, R. A., & Hungerford, H. (2017). Global citizenship in intercultural communication: Spatial awareness of globalization through map your consumption. *Communication Teacher, 31*(4), 220–225. doi:10.1080/17404622.2017.135838

Kwitonda, J. C. (2017). Development aid and disease discourse on display: The mutating techniques of neoliberalism. *Critical Discourse Studies, 14*(1), 23–38. doi:10.1080/17405904.2016.1174139

Lawless, B. (2016). Ally, friend, or mentor? Creating and maintaining effective cross-class alliances. *Journal of International and Intercultural Communication, 9*(4), 334–350. doi:10.1080/17513057.2016.1225443

Lawless, B. (2019). Street level learning: Transforming understandings of poverty through semi-structured pedagogies. *Journal of Poverty, 23*(7), 543–558. doi:10.1080/10875549.2019.1616034

Lawless, B., & Chen, Y.-W. (2015). Immigrant women, academic work, and agency: Negotiating identities and subjectivities with/in the ivory tower. *The International Journal of Diversity in Organizations, Communities, and Nations: Annual Review, 14,* 39–50.

Lawless, B., & Chen, Y.-W. (2017). Multicultural neoliberalism and academic labor: Experiences of female immigrant faculty in the U.S. academy, *17*(3), *Cultural Studies↔Critical Methodologies,* 236–243. doi:10.1177/1532708616672688

Lawless, B., & Chen, Y.-W. (2019). "You have to cry before you teach this class": Emotion with work and resistance in teaching intercultural communication. *Journal of Communication Pedagogy, 2,* 63–75. doi:10.31446/JCP.2019.14

Lawless, B., & Chen, Y.-W. (2020). Still a "sensitive" subject? Unpacking strengths and struggles of intercultural communication pedagogies. *Howard Journal of Communications,* 1–16. doi:10.1080/10646175.2019.1707135

Lawless, B., Rudick, C. K., & Golsan, K. (2019). Distinguishing (the) right from wrong: Knowledge, curriculum, and intellectual responsibility. *Communication Education, 68*(4), 481–495. doi:10.1080/03634523.2019.1645871

Lazos, S. (2012). Are student teaching evaluations holding back women and minorities? In G. Gutiérrez y Muhs, Y. F. Niemann, C. G. González, & A. P. Harris

(Eds.), *Presumed incompetent: The intersections of race and class for women in academia* (pp. 164–185). Boulder: University Press of Colorado.

Lea, V., & Sims, E. J. (2008). Introduction: Undoing Whiteness in the classroom: Different origins, shared commitment. *Counterpoints, 321*, 1–28.

Leeds-Hurwitz, W. (1990). Notes in the history of intercultural communication: The foreign service institute and the mandate for intercultural training. *Quarterly Journal of Speech, 76*, 262–281.

Lensmire, T. J., McManimon, S. K., Dockter Tierney, J., Lee-Nichols, M. E., Casey, Z. A., Lensmire, A., & Davis, B. M. (2013). McIntosh as synecdoche: How teacher education's focus on white privilege undermines antiracism. *Harvard Educational Review, 83*(3), 410–431. doi:10.17763/haer.83.3.35054h1418230574

Leonardo, Z. (2009). *Race, whiteness and education*. New York, NY: Routledge.

Loomba, A. (2005). *Colonialism/postcolonialism* (2nd ed.). London: Routledge.

Lopez Bunyasi, T., & Smith, C. W. (2019). *Stay woke: A people's guide to making all Black lives matter*. New York, NY: New York University Press.

Lorde, A. (2007). *Sister outsider: Essays and speeches by Audre Lorde*. Berkeley, CA: Crossing Press.

Love, B. L. (2019). *We want to do more than survive: Abolitionist teaching and the pursuit of educational freedom*. Boston, MA: Beacon Press.

Martin, J. N., & Davis, O. I. (2001). Conceptual foundations for teaching about whiteness in intercultural communication courses. *Communication Education, 50*(4), 298–313. doi:10.1080/03634520109379257

Martin, J. N., & Nakayama, T. K. (1999). Thinking dialectically about culture and communication. *Communication Theory, 9*(1), 1–25.

Martin, J. N., & Nakayama, T. K. (2010). Intercultural communication and dialectics revisited. In R. T. Halualani & T. K. Nakayama (Eds.), *The Handbook of Critical Intercultural Communication* (pp. 51–83). Malden, MA: Blackwell.

Martin, J. N., & Nakayama, T. K. (2018). *Intercultural communication in contexts*. New York, NY: McGraw-Hill.

McIntosh, D. D., Moon, D. G., & Nakayama, T. K. (Eds.). (2019). *Interrogating the communicative power of whiteness*. New York, NY: Routledge.

McIntosh, P. (1997). White privilege and male privilege: A personal account of coming to see correspondences through work in Women's Studies. In R. Delgado & J. Stefancic (Eds.), *Critical White Studies: Looking Behind the Mirror* (pp. 291–299). Philadelphia, PA: Temple University.

McKinney, K. D. (2008). Confronting young people's perceptions of whiteness: Privilege or liability? *Sociology Compass, 2*(4), 1303–1330. https://doi.org/10.1111/j.1751-9020.2008.00126.x

McLuhan, M. (2011). *The Gutenberg galaxy: The making of typographic man*. Toronto, Ontario, Canada: University of Toronto Press.

McNabb, N., & Friedman, R. (2009). Re-learning American history: Understanding the assumptions underlying intercultural communication. *Communication Teacher, 23*(1), 32–36. doi: 10.1080/17404620802592981

Mendoza, S. L. (2006). Tears in the archive: Creating memory to survive and to contest empire. In M. W. Lustig & J. Koester (Eds.), *Among US: Essays on identity, belonging, and intercultural competence* (2nd ed., pp. 233–245). Boston, MA: Allyn & Bacon.

Mendoza, S. L. (2010). Reflections on "Bridging paradigms: How not to throw out the baby of collective representation with the functionalist bathwater in critical intercultural communication." In T. K. Nakayama & R. T. Halualani (Eds.), *The Handbook of Critical Intercultural Communication* (pp. 98–111). Malden, MA: Wiley-Blackwell.

Mendoza, S. L., Halualani, R. T., & Drzewiecka, J. A. (2002). Moving the discourse on identities in intercultural communication: Structure, culture and resignifications. *Communication Quarterly, 50*, 312–327.

Meyer, U. (2007). In the name of identity: Teaching cultural awareness in the intercultural classroom. *Journal of Intercultural Communication, 19*, 3–3.

Miike, Y. (2006). Non-Western theory in Western research? An Asiacentric agenda for Asian Communication Studies. *Review of Communication, 6*(1–2), 4–31. doi:10.1080/15358590600763243

Miike, Y. (2007). An Asiacentric reflection on Eurocentric bias in communication theory. *Communication Monographs, 74*(2), 272–278.

Miller, K. E., & Wieland, M. (2019). Teaching metatheory through research application and design. *Communication Teacher, 33*, 21–25. doi:10.1080/17404622.2018.1530797

Moon, D. G. (1996). Concepts of "culture": Implications for intercultural communication research. *Communication Quarterly, 44*(1), 70–84.

Moon, D. G. (2010). Critical reflections on culture and critical intercultural communication. In T. K Nakayama & R. T. Halualani (Eds.), *The handbook of critical intercultural communication* (pp. 33–52). West Sussex, UK: Wiley-Blackwell.

Moon, D. G., & Holling, M. A. (2016). *Race(ing) intercultural communication: Racial logics in a colorblind era*. New York, NY: Routledge.

Moon, D. G., & Nakayama, T. K. (2005). Strategic social identities and judgments: A murder in Appalachia. *Howard Journal of Communications, 16*(2), 87–107. doi:10.1080/10646170590948965

Mudambi, A. (2015). The construction of brownness: Latino/a and South Asian bloggers' Responses to SB 1070. *Journal of International and Intercultural Communication, 8*(1), 44–62. doi:10.1080/17513057.2015.991079

Mumby, D. K. (1989). Ideology & the social construction of meaning: A communication perspective. *Communication Quarterly, 37*(4), 291–304. doi:10.1080/01463378909385551

Nagda, B. A. (2006). Breaking barriers, crossing borders, building bridges: Communication process in intergroup dialogues. *Journal of Social Issues, 62*(3), 553–576.

Nakayama, T. K., & Krizek, R. L. (1995). Whiteness: A strategic rhetoric. *Quarterly Journal of Speech, 81*, 291–309.

Nakayama, T. K., & Martin, J. N. (Eds.). (1999). *Whiteness: The communication of social identity*. Thousand Oaks, CA: SAGE.

Nakayama, T. K., & Martin, J. N. (2007). The "white problem" in intercultural communication research and pedagogy. In L. Cooks & J. S. Simpson (Eds.), *Whiteness, pedagogy, performance: Dis/placing race* (pp. 111–137). Lanham, MD: Lexington Books.

National Public Radio. (2020). Tracking the pandemic: How quickly is the coronavirus spreading state by state? Retrieved from https://www.npr.org/sections/health-shots/2020/03/16/816707182/map-tracking-the-spread-of-the-coronavirus-in-the-u-s

Ono, K. (1998). Problematizing "Nation" in intercultural communication research. In D. Tanno & A. González (Eds.), *International and intercultural communication annual: Communication and identity across cultures* (Vol. 21, pp. 122–145). Thousand Oaks, CA: SAGE.

Ong, A. (1999). *Flexible citizenship: The cultural logics of transnationality*. Durham, MD: Duke University Press.

Pierce, C. (1974). Psychiatric problems of the black minority. In S. Arietie (Ed.), *American handbook of psychiatry* (pp. 512–523). New York, NY: Basic Books.

Quijada, D. A. (2008). Reconciling research, rallies, and citizenship: Reflections on youth-led diversity workshops and intercultural alliances. *Social Justice, 35*(1), 76–90.

Rich, M. D., & Cargile, A. C. (2004). Beyond the breach: Transforming white identities in the classroom. *Race Ethnicity and Education, 7*(4), 351–365. doi:10.1080/1361332042000303379

Rodríguez, C. O. (2018). *Decolonizing academia: Poverty, oppression, and pain*. Nova Scotia, Canada: Fernwood Publishing.

Roksa, J., Arum, R., & Cook, A. (2016). Defining and assessing learning in higher education. In R. Arum, J. Roksa, & A. Cook (Eds.), *Improving quality in American higher education: Learning outcomes and assessments for the 21st century* (pp. 1–36). San Francisco, CA: Jossey-Bass.

Rowe, D. D., Rudnick, J. J., & White, L. (2019). Images of identity: Performing power and intersectionality. *Communication Teacher, 34*(4), 1–8. doi:10.1080/17404622.2019.1690156

Saad, L. (2020). *Me and white supremacy: Combatting racism, changing the world, and becoming a good ancestor*. Naperville, IL: Sourcebooks.

Sekimoto, S., & Brown, C. (2016). A phenomenology of the racialized tongue: Embodiment, language, and the bodies that speak. *Departures in Critical Qualitative Research, 5*(2), 101–122. doi:10.1525/dcqr.2016.5.2.101

Shome, R. (2003). Space matters: The powerful and practice of space. *Communication Theory, 13*, 39–56.

Shome, R., & Hegde, R. S. (2002). Postcolonial approaches to communication: Charting the terrain, engaging the intersections. *Communication Theory, 12*(3), 249–270.

Shor, I. (1993). Education is politics: Paulo Freire's critical pedagogy. In P. McLaren & P. Leonard (Eds.), *Paulo Freire: A critical encounter* (pp. 24–35). New York, NY: Routledge.

Shuter, R. (2012). Intercultural new media studies: The next frontier in intercultural communication. *Journal of Intercultural Communication Research, 41*(3), 219–237. doi:10.1080/17475759.2012.728761

Simmons, N. (2014). "We're a culture, not a costume": Ethical analysis of a college student-led organization's anti-racism campaign. *Public Voices, 14*(1), 97–114. doi: http://dx.doi.org/10.22140/pv.23

Simmons, N., & Chen, Y. W. (2014). Using six-word memoirs to increase cultural identity awareness. *Communication Teacher, 28*(1), 20–25. doi:10.1080/17404622.2013.839050

Simpson, J. L. (2008). The color-blind double bind: Whiteness and the (im)possibility of dialogue. *Communication Theory, 18*, 139–159. doi:10.1111=j.1468-2885.2007.00317.x

Simpson, J. S., Causey, A., & Williams, L. (2007). "I would want you to understand it": Students' perspectives on addressing race in the classroom. *Journal of Intercultural Communication Research, 36*(1), 33–50. doi: 10.1080/17475750701265274

Smith, A. G. (1982). Content decisions in intercultural communication. *Southern Speech Communication Journal, 47*(3), 252–262. doi:10.1080/10417948209372531

Smith, W. A. (2004). Black faculty coping with racial battle fatigue: The campus racial climate in a post-civil rights era. In D. Cleveland (Ed.), *A long way to go: Conversations about race by African American faculty and graduate students* (pp. 171–192). New York, NY: Peter Lang.

Solorzano, D. G. (1998). Critical race theory, race and gender microaggressions, and the experience of Chicana and Chicano scholars. *Qualitative Studies in Education, 11*(1), 121–136.

Solorzano, D., Ceja, M., & Yosso, T. (2000). Critical race theory, racial microaggressions, and campus racial climate: The experiences of African American college students. *Journal of Negro Education, 69*(1), 60–73.

Sorrells, K. (2010). Re-imagining intercultural communication in the context of globalization. In T. K. Nakayama & R. T. Halualani (Eds.), *The handbook of critical intercultural communication* (pp. 171–189). Malden, MA: Blackwell.

Sorrells, K. (2013). Negotiating intercultural conflict and social justice. *Intercultural communication: Globalization and social justice*. Thousand Oaks, CA: SAGE.

Sorrells, K. (2016). *Intercultural communication: Globalization and social justice* (2nd ed.). Los Angeles, CA: SAGE.

Sorrells, K., & Nakagawa, G. (2008). Intercultural communication praxis and the struggle for social responsibility and social justice. In O. Swartz (Ed.), *Transformative communication studies: Culture, hierarchy, and the human condition* (pp. 17–43). Leicester, UK: Troubador Publishing.

Stewart, D-L. (2017, March 30). Language of appeasement. *Inside Higher Ed*. Retrieved from https://www.insidehighered.com/views/2017/03/30/colleges-need-language-shift-not-one-you-think-essay

Stewart, D.-L. (2018). Minding the gap between diversity and institutional transformation: Eight proposals for enacting institutional change. *Teachers College Record, 120*(14), 1–16.

Stringer, D. M., & Cassiday, P. A. (2009). *52 activities for improving cross-cultural communication*. Boston, MA: Intercultural Press.

Swartz, D. (1997). *Culture & power: The sociology of Pierre Bourdieu*. Chicago, IL: The University of Chicago Press.

Tanno, D. (2016). Names, narratives, and the evolution of ethnic identity. In A. González & Y-W. Chen (Eds.), *Our voices: Essays in culture, ethnicity, and communication, 5e* (pp. 44–47). New York, NY: Oxford University Press.

Tierney, S., & Jackson, R. L., II. (2003). Deconstructing whiteness ideology as a set of rhetorical fantasy themes: Implications for interracial alliance building in the United States. In M. J. Collier (Ed.), *Intercultural alliances: Critical transformation* (pp. 81–106). Thousand Oaks, CA: SAGE.

Ting-Toomey, S. (2003). Communicative resourcefulness: An identity negotiation perspective. In R. Wiseman & J. Koester (Eds.), *Intercultural communication competence*. Newbury Park, CA: SAGE.

Toyosaki, S., & Eguchi, S. (Eds.). (2017). *Intercultural communication in Japan: Theorizing homogenizing discourse*. New York, NY: Routledge.

van Dijk, T. A. (1998). *Ideology: A multidisciplinary approach*. London: SAGE.

Wander, P. C., Nakayama, T., & Martin, J. (1999). Whiteness and beyond: Sociohistorical foundations of whiteness and contemporary challenges. In T. Nakayama & J. Martin (Eds.), *Whiteness: The communication of social identity* (pp. 13–26). Thousand Oaks, CA: SAGE.

Warren, J. T. (2010). It really isn't about you: Whiteness and the dangers of thinking you got it. In T. K. Nakayama & R. T. Halualani (Eds.), *The handbook of critical intercultural communication* (pp. 446–460). West Sussex, UK: Wiley-Blackwell.

West, C. (2001). *Race matters*. Boston, MA: Beacon Press Books.

World Health Organization. (2020). WHO director-general's opening remarks at the media briefing on COVID-19—March 5, 2020. Retrieved from https://www.who.int/dg/speeches/detail/who-director-general-s-opening-remarks-at-the-media-briefing-on-covid-19-5-march-2020

Yep, G. A. (2010). Foreword. In P. Backland & G. Wakefield (Eds.), *A communication assessment primer* (p. vii). Washington, DC: National Communication Association. Retrieved from https://www.natcom.org/sites/default/files/pages/Assessment_Resources_ A_Communication_Assessment_Primer.pdf

Yep, G. A., & Lescure, R. M. (2018). Obstructing the process of becoming: Basal whiteness and the challenge to critical intercultural communication pedagogy. In A. Atay & S. Toyosaki (Eds.), *Critical intercultural communication pedagogy* (pp. 115–136). Lanham, MD: Lexington Books.

Zompetti, J. P. (2006). Embracing a critical communication pedagogy: A radical examination of the common communication course. *Radical Pedagogy*, *8*(2), 4–4.

Index

Note: Page numbers in *italics* refers to illustrations.

access, to resources, 13, 66, 67
accomplice, ally contrasted with, 58
acting and thinking globally, 12, 89–100
activism, 67–68; power through, 35; for social change, 13
activity: alliance, 62, 152–54; avowed and ascribed identity, 51, 131; community observation, 73–74; consumption, 99; cultural pyramid, 51, 129–30; "The Phone at the End of the World," 99; Refugee Olympic Team, 99; service learning journal, 74; six-word memoir, 51; wall, 25
Adams, M., 4–5
additional training, for teaching intercultural communication, 117
advantage, unearned, 32, 38
affirmation, of avowed identities, 58
African American, 63, 81, 114
Afrocentricity (Asante), 75, 81
Ahmed, S., 4
Alcoff, L. M., 58
Alexander, B. K., 4, 5, 75
Allen, B. J., 29
Allen, R. L., 78
alliance activities, 62, 152–54
alliances: building, 11, 55–63; intergroup, 61

allies, racial, 55–56, 60–61, 117–18
"Ally or accomplice? The language of activism" (Clemens), 58
American commodities in an age of empire (Domosh), 81–82
the American Dream, as myth, 87
analysis, frames for, *66*
Anderson, B., 91
anti-immigrant discourse, 69
anti-intellectualism, 70
Appadurai, A., 90; dimensions of globalization of, 91–92
application of critical assessment, to intercultural communication, 102–3
application of knowledge, in community engagement, 72–73
approaches, to teaching intercultural communication, 17
Arasaratnam, L. A., 4, 5, 75
archaeology, power and, 31
The Archaeology of Knowledge and the Discourse of Language (Foucault), 31
"Are student teaching evaluations holding back women and minorities?" (Lazos), 108
"Are You Upholding White Supremacy?" (Lopez Bunyasi & Smith, C. W.), 86–87

articulation of philosophies, and assumptions, 10, 17–26
Asante, Godfried, 75, 81, 85–86, 92–93
ascribed identities, 43, 44–45, 50–51
Ashby-King, D. T., 83
Asiacentricity, 82
Asian Americans, 49, 69
assessment, of intercultural pedagogies, 101–10
assessment plan, creation of, 104
assumptions, about heritage, 50
Atay, A., 7, 28, 89, 92
author backgrounds: of Chen, 1, 2, 36–37, 67, 89–90, 113, 114; of Lawless, 1, 44–45, 67, 69, 90
avowed and ascribed identity activity, 51, 131
avowed identities, 43, 44, 49, 50–51; affirmation of, 58

background: community engagement, 65–66; deconstruction of ideologies, 76–77; identity, 42; intercultural alliances, 56–57; pedagogy of intercultural communication, 17; power privilege and, 28
Baldwin, J. R, 7
Bardhan, N., 41
basal whiteness, 80
"The bases of social power" (French & Raven), 28–29
"Basic course central student learning outcomes" (Kahl), 102
battle fatigue, "cultural," 113–14
belief, in the individual, 85
Between the World and Me (Coates), 52
biases, exposing, 68, 69
biological determinism *vs.* social determinism, 45
Black Activism Is Changing Your Community for the Better (Blain), 74
"Black faculty coping with racial battle fatigue" (Smith, W. A.), 114
Black identities, 30, 33, 41, 44, 117
Black Lives Matter Movement, 48, 68, 97–98, 117–18

Blain, Cicely-Belle, 74
Blanton, Becky, 53
Blithe, S. J., 69
Bloom's Taxonomy, *103–4*
Boler, M., 31, 111, 114–15
Bourdieu, Pierre, 29
"Bridging paradigms" (Mendoza), 17, 20
Brown, C., 21
building alliances, 11, 55–63

Calafell, B. M., 114
campus constraints, to community engagement, 70–71
CAP. *See* communication activism pedagogy (CAP)
Carrillo Rowe, A. M., 27, 79
Census, use of Hispanic, 48
Central problems in social theory (Giddens), 77
challenges: of community engagement, 69–70; of critical course assessment, 107–8; of deconstruction of ideologies, 84–85; of discussions of identity, 44–45; of global citizenship engagement and, 96–97; to individualistic tendencies, 96; institutional, 36, 113; of intercultural alliances, 59–60; of multiparadigmatic approach to intercultural communication, 23; to social justice pedagogy, 33–37, 112–13
Chauvin, Derek, 109
CIT. *See* cultural identity theory (CIT)
citizenship, flexible, 95
class participation, 34–35; as positive or negative, 15
class privilege, contrasted with white privilege, 32–33
classroom, as neutral, 84
Clemens, Colleen, 58
closing the loop, on assessment, 106–7
Coates, Ta-Nehisi, 52
coercive power, 30
Coleman, R. R. M., 7
collaboration, multiparadigmatic, 20

Collier, Mary Jane: on avowed and ascribed identities, 43; on intercultural alliances, 11, 55, 57; on intercultural praxis, 95–96; on paradigms of intercultural communication, 20–21
colonial histories, of U.S. and Ghana, 85–86
colonialism, 15, 81–82, 85–86, 92; symbols of, 97–98. *See also* postcolonialism
colonialism/postcolonialism (Loomba), 77
colonized subjects, 81
The Color of Water (McBride), 52
Columbus, Christopher, 92
commencement, UC Berkeley, 94
communication: CHANGE, 59; least and most resistance paths of, 48; of power and privilege, 10–11, 27; qualitative methods, 21; as transmissive, 16
communication activism pedagogy (CAP), 67
A communication assessment primer (Yep), 101
Communication Teacher (journal), 10, 69
"Communicative resourcefulness" (Ting-Toomey), 42–43
communities, observation of, 73–74, 155–56
community-engaged learning, 68–69, 161n1
community engagement, 11, 13, 65–66, 121–23; application of knowledge in, 72–73; campus constraints to, 70–71; projects for, 106; savior complex in, 68–69
community partners, for engagement, 71
concept, of power, 28–29
"Conceptual foundations for teaching about whiteness in intercultural communication courses" (Martin & Davis, O. I.), 77–78
conferred dominance, 32
confronting historical trauma, 57–58

Confucius, philosophy of, 9
connections, between local and global, 96–97
consumption activity, 99
"Content decisions in intercultural communication" (Smith, A. G.), 7
contextual factors, in intercultural alliances, 61
control, through trade, 82
Cooks, L., 65, 77
Core concepts for social justice education (Adams & Zúñiga), 4–5
course concepts, lack of measurability, 108
course content: determining, *22*; on intercultural communication, 132–40, *140–41*, 143–47, *147–48*
Covarrubias, P. O., 21, 46–47
COVID-19, 89–90, 94–95, 96
creation, of assessment plan, 104
Crenshaw, Kimberlé, 33–34
critical assessment *vs.* traditional assessment, 102
"Critical communication pedagogy and assessment" (Kahl), 101–3, 108
critical intercultural communication, 6–7, 28
Critical Intercultural Communication Pedagogy (Atay & Toyosaki), 7, 28
"Critical intercultural communication studies" (Nakayama & Halualani), 17, 27
critical pedagogy, 2
"Critical race theory, race and gender microaggressions, and the experience of Chicana and Chicano scholars" (Solarzano), 58–59
critical reflection, on globalization, 90
critical turn, of intercultural communication studies, 6
"cultural" battle fatigue, 113–14
cultural identity, 42–43, 45; pyramid activity of, 51, 129–30
cultural identity theory (CIT), 43
Culturally Relevant Pedagogy (Howard, T. C.), 104
cultural politics of immigration, 93

culture, 18; biases in, 80–81; capital of, 29; identity and, 11, 23, 41–43; beyond nation-state, 5
curriculum development, 14

Dancing with Difference (Collier), 20–21, 55
Darder, A., 84
Davis, O. I., 77–78
Davis, R. W., 7
"Deconstructing whiteness ideology as a set of rhetorical fantasy themes" (Tierney & Jackson), 79
deconstruction, of ideologies, 12, 75–88
deconstruction, of white supremacy, 78
"Defining and communicating what "intercultural" and "intercultural communication" means to us" (Alexander, Arasaratnam, Flores, et al.), 4, 5, 75
definitions, complex, 18
defund the police movement, 118
delineation, racial, 48
Denzin, N. K., 21
determinism, biological *vs.* social, 45
DeTurk, Sara, 72–73
development, of curriculum, 14
"Development aid and disease discourse on display" (Kwitonda), 83
dialectical approach, to intercultural communication, 18
dialogue events, 72, 154
Dialogue Institute of the Southwest, 72
DiAngelo, R., 35
Difference matters (Allen, B.), 29
difficult topics, teaching, 8, 12, 15–16, 36–37, 115
difficulty, of studying white supremacy, 79
discourse, anti-immigrant, 69
discussions, ground rules for, 35, 47
"Diverging discourses" (Ashby-King, & Hanasono), 83
diversity: exploring, 51; language of, *19*, 25–26; as problematic term, 4–5,

83–84, 118; social justice contrasted with, 2, 3, 4–5, 25–26
dominance: conferred, 32; sociology of, 35
Domosh, M., 81–82
Drzewiecka, J. A., 43
Durham, A., 4, 5

"Education is politics" (Shor), 75–76
Eguchi, S., 92
embodied state, of cultural capital, 29
emotional labor, 1, 112, 115–16
empire, United States (U.S.) as, 81
engagement, community, 11, 13, 65–66, 121–23
epistemologies, Western-centered, 23
equity, 3, 4–5
Eurocentric cultural assumptions, 80–81
events, dialogue, 72
everyday thinking, power and privilege in, 28
exams, open-ended, 106
experience: instructors with, 8, 14; with race, 52; of teaching social justice, 12, 36–37
expert power, 30
exposure, of biases, 68

Feeling power (Boler), 31, 111, 114–15
feeling privileged, 33
flexible citizenship, 95
Flores, L., 75, 93
Floyd, George, 109
fluid, identities as, 49–50
Foreign Service Institute (FSI), 6
Foucault, Michel, 31
fragility, white, 35
frames for analysis, *66*
Francis, Megan Ming, 39
free-write journals, 106
French, J. R. P., Jr., 28–29, 30
Frey, L. R., 65, 67, 68
friendships *vs.* intercultural alliances, *56*
FSI. *See* Foreign Service Institute (FSI)

Ghana, 85–86
Giddens, Anthony, 77
global and local, connection between, 96–97
globalization, 92, 97–98, 118; critical reflection on, 90; imagined worlds as, 91
"The globalization of white supremacy" (Allen, R.), 78
Globalization's impact on cultural identity formation (Atay), 89
globally, thinking and acting, 12, 89–100
global white supremacy, 78
glocalized whiteness, 92–93
González, Alberto, 7, 49–50
Griffin, R. A., 78, 111
ground rules, for discussions, 35, 47
group membership, 48
"guide on the side," teacher as, 9
The Gutenberg Galaxy (McLuhan), 91

Hall, Edward, 49
Halualani, R. T., 17, 27, 43
Hanasono, L. K., 83
harmful: assumptions, 50; communication scenarios, 46–47; ideologies, 16
Hegde, R. S., 82, 89, 90
The Help (film), 78
Hendrix, K. G., 27
heritage, 50
"(Un)hinging whiteness" (Carrillo Rowe & Malhotra), 79
Hispanic, Census use of, 48
historical context, of identities, 45
historical trauma, consulting, 57–58
histories, colonial, of U.S. and Ghana, 85
history, of marginalized groups, 57
Hofstede, Geert, 49
hooks, b., 41
Howard, G. R., 47
Howard, T. C., 104
How to be an antiracist (Kendi), 35
Huang (Mr.), 9
humanism, liberal, 85
hurtful comment, response to, 46–47, 47–48

ideas, marketplace of, 3, 36; anti-intellectualism in, 70
identifications, contrasted with identities, 43
identities, 11, 41, 53; ascribed, 43, 44–45, 50–51; avowed, 43, 44, 50–51; Black, 30, 33, 41, 44, 117; culture and, 23, 42–43; as fluid, 49–50; historical context of, 45; identifications contrasted with, 43; as intersectional, 44; perspectives on, 43–44; progression of, 49–50; reflection in class reading of, 47; reflection on, 44; resources and, 13; as stable, 49–50; Western Society view on, 42
Identity research and communication (Bardhan & Orbe), 41
ideologies, 76, 77; deconstruction of, 12, 75; harmful, 16
Imagined communities (Anderson), 91
imagined worlds, globalization as, 91
immigrants: Mexican, 93; negative discourse about, 69; undocumented, 84
immigration, cultural politics of, 93
imperialism, Western/European/U.S., 80–83
individual, belief in, 85
inequities, reflection on, 110, 113
influence of stereotypes, on student evaluations, 108
institutional challenges, of discussing social justice, 36, 113
institutionalized form, of cultural capital, 30
instructors, of intercultural communication, 1, 4, *157*; experienced, 14; as "guide on the side," 9; new, 13; privilege and, 36–37
intercultural alliances, 56; friendships vs., 56; three tenets of, 57–58
intercultural communication: additional training for, 117; application of critical assessment to, 102–3; approaches to, 17, 18, *19*; as battleground, 114;

challenges of teaching, 112; courses on, 132–40, *140–41*, 143–47, *147–48*; critical, 6–7; critical turn of, 6; instructors of, 1, 4; interaction activity of, 52; paradigms for study of, 18–19, *19*, 24–25; pedagogy of, 7, 12; reading circles for, 52; relatable theories *vs.* activist approaches, 67; relationships in, 55; as required course, 2–3, 6, 7; scholars of, 5; social justice and, 6; stereotypes, 49; student learning objectives for, 103–4. *See also specific topics*
Intercultural Communication (Sorrells), 7, 66, 89, 91
"Intercultural communication, ethics, and activism pedagogy" (Cooks), 65
"Intercultural communication and dialectics revisited" (Martin & Nakayama), 20
Intercultural Communication for Everyday Life (Baldwin, Coleman, González & Shenoy-Packer), 7
Intercultural Communication for Global Engagement (Davis, R. W., & Patterson-Masuka), 7
Intercultural Communication in Contexts (Martin & Nakayama), 18
Intercultural communication in Japan (Toyosaki & Eguchi), 92
"Intercultural communication praxis and the struggle for social responsibility and social justice" (Sorrells & Nakagawa), 95
intercultural conflict retreat, 60–61
intercultural encounters, reflections on, 109
"Intercultural new media studies" (Shuter), 94
intercultural praxis, points of, 95
intergroup alliances, 61
interpragmatic approaches, to teaching, 20–23
intersectional: identity as, 44; privilege as, 33–34
Islamophobia, 53
"It Really Isn't about You" (Warren, J. T.), 84–85

Jackson, R. L., 27, 79
Johnson, A. G., 33, 48
journals, free-write, 106

Kahl, D. H., Jr., 101–3, 108
Kawai, Y., 83
Kendi, I. X., 35
Kennerly, R. M., 69
Krizek, R. L., 78, 79
Kwitonda, J. C., 83

labor, emotional, 1, 112, 115–16
lack of measurability, of course concepts, 108
language: Bloom's Taxonomy and, 103–4; of diversity, *19*, 25–26; nature of, 45; power relations and, 29
Latina, 15
Latinx people, 30, 50
Lazos, S., 108
Lea, V., 80
learning, community-based, 68–69, 161n1
least and most resistance, paths of communication, 48
legitimate power, 30
Leonardo, Z., 34, 79
Lescure, R. M., 80
liberal humanism, 85
liberal pluralism, 20
local and global, connections between, 96–97
Loomba, A., 77
Lopez Bunyasi, T., 86–87
Lorde, Andre, 34

macro-frame, 66
Malhotra, S., 79
"Mapping the margins" (Crenshaw), 33–34
marginalized groups, history of, 57
marginalized voices, recentering of, 47
marketplace of ideas, 3, 36; anti-intellectualism in, 70
Martin, J. N., 18, 20, 77–78, 79–80
"Masked silence sequences" (Covarrubias), 21, 46–47
McBride, James, 52
McIntosh, Peggy, 32–33

McLuhan, M., 91
media, right-wing, 1
meeting, town hall, 61
membership, in groups, 48
Mendoza, S. L., 17, 20, 43, 75, 81
mentorship, 116–17, *157*
metatheory, teaching, 25
methods, of teaching, 8–10
Mexican Americans, 50
Mexican immigrants, 93
microaggressions, 48, 51, 55, 58–59, 62, 150–51
micro-level communication, 11, 12
Miike, Y., 82
minority students, 116
Modernity at large (Appadurai), 90
Mogahed, Dalia, 53
"Moving the discourse on identities in intercultural communication" (Mendoza, Halualani & Drzewiecka), 43
Mudambi, Anjana, 27, 37–38
multiculturalism, neoliberal, 84
multicultural/multiracial Obama-ism, 80
multiparadigmatic collaboration, in intercultural communication: challenges of, 20
Muslims, 53; women, 84
myth, American Dream as, 87

Nakayama, T. K.: on pedagogies of intercultural communication, 17, 18, *19*, 20; on power privilege and, 27; on white supremacy, 78, 79–80
National Communication Association: assessment primer, 107; objectives, 103
nation-state, culture beyond, 6
Native American perspective, on Washington Redskins, 37
nature, of language, 45
"Negotiating intercultural alliance relationships" (Collier), 57
neoliberalism, 3, 83–84
"Neoliberalism, nationalism, and intercultural communication" (Kawai), 83
"Neoliberalism in the academic borderlands" (Darder), 84

neoliberal multiculturalism, 84
new media, 93–94
new technology, role of students in, 94
Nina G. (comedian), 62
"Non-Western theory in Western research?" (Miike), 82

Obama presidency, 79–80, 112
objectified state, of cultural capital, 29–30
obliviousness, about white privilege, 32
observation, of communities, 73–74, 155–56
"Obstructing the process of becoming" (Yep & Lescure), 80
Ono, K., 93
open-ended exams, 106
Orbe, M. P., 41
orientation, of affirmation, 58

Palestine, 98
Palmer, D. L., 65, 67, 68
papers, reflection, 106
paradigmatic approaches to intercultural communication, *19*
paradigm purism, 21–22
paradigms: in intercultural communication research, 24–25, 26; for study of intercultural communication, 18–19, *19*
paradox, privilege as, 33
Parnell, Whitney, 63
participation, in class, 15, 34–35
paths of most and least resistance, of communication, 48
Patterson-Masuka, A., 7
peaceCENTER, San Antonio, 72
pedagogical activities: class assessment in, 110; community engagement in, 73–74; deconstruction of ideologies in, 86–87; global thought in, 99–100; identity exploration as, 51–52; intercultural alliances in, 62–63; paradigms intercultural communication of, 24–26; power and privilege exposed through, 38–39
pedagogical praxis, 111
perspectives, on identity, 43–44

"A phenomenology of the racialized tongue" (Sekimoto & Brown), 21
philosophies and assumptions, articulation of, 10
philosophy of Confucius, 9
"The Phone at the End of the World" activity, 99
pluralism, liberal, 20
policy change, through activism, 35
politics, in intercultural communication, 67, 70, 75, 116, 161n2
"Postcolonial approaches to communication" (Shome & Hegde), 82, 89, 90
postcolonialism, 19, 82
power, 28–30; through activism, 35; language and, 29; privilege and, 10–11, 31–34, 36–39, 57, 118
Power lines (Carillo Rowe), 27
power-with and power-over, 31
praxis: intercultural, 95; pedagogical, 111; social justice based on, 94–95
privilege, 124–28; discussing, 34–37; feeling of, 33; as intersectional, 33–34; as paradox, 33; status quo and, 28; white, 14, 15, 32–33, 109
Privilege, power, and difference (Johnson), 33, 48
privileged backgrounds, students from, 36
"Problematic representations of strategic whiteness and "postracial" pedagogy" (Griffin), 78, 111
"Problematizing "Nation" in intercultural communication research" (Ono), 93
"The problem of speaking for others" (Alcoff), 58
problems, with term "diversity", 4–5
progression, of identities, 49–50
projects, for community engagement, 106
purism, paradigm, 21–22
pyramid, of culture, 51, 129–30

The Qualitative Manifesto (Denzin), 21
qualitative methods, in communication, 21

race, as social construct, 48
Race, whiteness and education (Leonardo), 34, 79

racial allies, 55–56, 60–61, 117–18
racial delineation, 48
racialization, 46–47
racism: structural, 14–15, 37, 92; systemic, 28, 67, 68, 78, 109–10
Raven, B., 28–29, 30
reading circles, intercultural, 52
re-centering, of marginalized voices, 47
referent power, 30
reflection: on experience with race, 52; of identities in class reading, 47; on inequities, 110; on intercultural encounters, 109; papers, 106; on quality of teaching, 108–9; on teaching identity, 44, 46–48
Refugee Olympic Team, 99
relatable theories, of intercultural communication *vs.* activist approaches, 67–68
relations, power, 28
relationships: with heritage, 50; in intercultural communication, 55; student-teacher, 16
reliance, on student evaluations, 108
required course, intercultural communication as, 2–3, 6, 7
resistance, against harmful ideologies, 16
resources, access to, 13, 66, 67
response, to hurtful comment, 46–47, 47–48
retreat, intercultural conflict, 60–61
reward power, 30
rhetoric, of whiteness, 78–79
right-wing media, 1
role, of students, in new technology, 94

sample student learning outcomes, *105*
savior complex, in community engagement, 68–69
scholars, of intercultural communication, 5
Sekimoto, S., 21
self, sense of, 42
self-care, 116, *116*
self-reflexivity, 49
sense, of self, 42
sensitive topics, 5, 8

"Service-learning, intercultural communication, and video production praxis" (Kennerly), 69
service learning journal activity, 74
shared recognition, of histories, 57–58
Shenoy-Packer, S., 7
"Shifting academic landscapes" (Hendrix, Jackson & Warren, J. R.), 27
Shome, R., 82, 89, 90
Shor, I., 75–76
Shukla, Pratibha, 9
Shuter, R., 94
Sims, E. J., 80
Sister outsider (Lorde), 34
six-word memoir activity, 51
skin tanning *vs.* skin bleaching, 85–86
SLOs. *See* Student Learning Objectives (SLOs), in intercultural communication
Smith, A. G., 7
Smith, C. W., 86–87
Smith, W. A., 114
social change, activism for, 13
social construct, race as, 48
social construction, of whiteness, 46
social constructionism *vs.* biological determinism, 45
social justice: contrasted with diversity, 2, 3, 4–5, 25–26; praxis-based, 94–95. *See also specific topics*
sociology of dominance, 35
Solorzano, D. G., 58–59
Sorrells, Kathryn: on community engagement, 66; on globalization, 89, 91, 92, 95, 97–98; on paradigms of intercultural communication, 7
status quo, and privilege, 28, 70
Stay Woke (Lopez Bunyasi & Smith, C. W.), 86–87
Stewart, D-L., 5
stories from the field: on community engagement, 72–73; on course assessment, 109–10; on identity, 48–51; on intercultural alliances, 60–62; on paradigms of intercultural communication, 24–25; on power and privilege, 37–38
Street Retreats, 69
structural racism, 14–15, 37
student evaluations, reliance on, 108
Student Learning Objectives (SLOs), in intercultural communication, 103–4
student perceptions, to community engagement, 71
students: from privileged backgrounds, 36–37; use of power to reach, 37–38
student-teacher relationships, 16, 36
subjects, colonized, 81
supremacy, white, 46, 77, 92; deconstruction of, 78; difficulty of studying, 79; global, 78–79
SWAPping, 45–46
symbolic power, 29
symbols, of colonialism, 98
systemic racism, 28, 67, 68, 78, 109–10

Taiwan, 2, 9
taken-for-granted beliefs, value systems and, 84
Tanno, Dolores V., 49
Taxonomy of Bloom, *103–4*
teachers. *See* instructors
teaching: approaches to, 17, 18, *19*; challenges of, 112–13; difficult topics, 8, 12, 15–16, 36–37, 115; interpragmatic approaches to, 20–23; metatheory of, 25; methods of, 8–10; reflection on quality of, 108; time constraints in, 8, 12, 15–16; videos for, 26, 39, 53, 62–63, 74, 87, 100
Teaching communication activism (Frey & Palmer), 65, 67, 68
"Teaching critical moments within neoliberal universities" (Chen & Lawless), 67
"Teaching intercultural communication through service-learning" (Blithe), 69
"Tears in the archive" (Mendoza), 81
the Tenderloin district, San Francisco, 68
"Theorizing cultural identifications" (Collier), 43

"think globally, act locally," 97
"thinking and acting g(locally)," 98–99
"Thinking dialectically about culture and communication" (Martin & Nakayama), 18
three tenets of intercultural alliances, 57–58
Tierney, S., 79
time constraints, in teaching, 23
Ting-Toomey, S., 42–43
Tío, Adrian, 50
topics, sensitive, 5, 8
town hall meeting, 61
Toyosaki, S., 7, 28, 92
trade, control through, 82
traditional assessment *vs.* critical assessment, 102, 107–8
training, for intercultural communication, 117
transmissive communication, 16
Trump, Donald J., 98
Trump Administration, 84, 113
2010 Census, 48

UC Berkeley commencement, 94
undocumented immigrants, 84
"Undoing Whiteness in the classroom" (Lea & Sims), 80
unearned advantage, 32, 38
United States (U.S.), as empire, 81
universities and colleges: diversity preferred over social justice by, 2–3, 4
U.S. *See* United States (U.S.)

value systems, taken-for-granted beliefs and, 84
Vargas, Jose Antonio, 53
videos, as teaching tools: community engagement, 74; deconstruction of ideologies in, 87; globalization, 100; identity, 53; intercultural alliances, 62–63; paradigms of intercultural communication, 26; power and privilege in, 39

wall activity, 25
Warren, J. R., 27
Warren, J. T., 84–85
Washington Redskins, 37–38
We can't teach what we don't know (Howard, G. R.), 47
Western-centered epistemologies, 23
Western/European/U.S. Imperialism, 80–83
Western society, view of identity, 42
"When will we all matter?" (Calafell), 114
white fragility, 35
White fragility (DiAngelo), 35
whiteness: glocalized, 92–93; social construction of, 46; as strategic rhetoric, 78–79
"Whiteness" (Nakayama, & Krizek), 78, 79
white privilege, 14, 15, 109; class privilege contrasted with, 32–33
"White Privilege and Male Privilege" (McIntosh), 32–33
"The 'white problem' in intercultural communication research and pedagogy" (Nakayama & Martin), 78
white supremacy, 46, 77, 92; deconstruction of, 78; difficulty of studying, 79; global, 78–79
Wise, Tim, 39
women, Muslim, 84

Yearning race, gender, and cultural politics (hooks), 41
Yep, Gust, 48–49, 80, 101

Zúñiga, X., 4–5

About the Authors

Brandi Lawless is an associate professor and chair of the Department of Communication Studies at the University of San Francisco. She earned her MA degree from the San Francisco State University and PhD degree from the University of New Mexico. Her primary area of research is Critical Intercultural Communication Pedagogy. Her research explores the intersections of race, class, gender, and nationality in a variety of contexts in higher education and nonprofit contexts. Her work appears in *Journal of International and Intercultural Communication*, *Journal of Applied Communication Research*, *Communication Education*, *Howard Journal of Communication*, *Critical Studies ⇔ Cultural Methodologies*, *Women's Studies in Communication, Journal of Communication Pedagogy,* and *Communication Teacher* as well as several edited collections. In 2015, she won the USF Innovation in Teaching with Technology Award. In 2016, she won the USF Distinguished Teaching Award. She is also the recipient of numerous top paper awards at regional, national, and international conferences.

Yea-Wen Chen is an associate professor in the School of Communication, director of the Institute for Dialogue and Social Justice, and director of Faculty International Engagement at San Diego State University. She earned her MA degree from the University of North Texas and PhD degree from the University of New Mexico. She previously served as a professor of equity co-facilitating seminars on equity, implicit bias, and microaggressions on her campus. Her research examines how communication—including silence—about cultural identities impacts diversity, inclusion, and social justice across contexts such as identity-based nonprofit organizations. She is the winner of numerous top paper awards at regional, national, and international communication conferences. Dr. Chen has published over forty works, including peer-reviewed articles in *Journal of International and Intercultural Communication*, *Journal of Intercultural Communication Research*, and *Departures in Critical Qualitative Research*.